303406

• Contents

CONTENTS

Introduction

Early morning at low tide on the River Thames . . . a waterman calls through the mist across the water; do you want a boat? It is barely dawn, and you can see candlelight moving about in a house close by as the day begins. Behind you is the town, still dark; ahead the newly opened Globe Theatre stands ready on the south bank – for it is 1599 and a play by William Shakespeare will open there today.

If you could make such a journey through time, on such a day, what a different world you'd see: sixteenth-century London waking up to its narrow bustling streets filled with pedlars and children darting between stalls. You might glimpse and hurry past a dank and smelly alley filled with dirt and sewage, a run for deadly rats, carrying the plague. You'd be hustled and pressed by courtiers, merchants, adventurers and vagabonds, journeymen and water-carriers, craftsmen and beggars, some on their way to the gallows, or the bear-pit – or the Globe.

Tudor London had much that someone from medieval times would have recognised, but the Globe Theatre was built in the new world of the Renaissance – the time of a 'new birth'. Vagabonds from another parish would still be crying in the streets, branded with a 'V' and cruelly flogged back to where they came from. But apothecaries were creating new medicines to make the sick better, experimenting with curious substances come all the way from America and the mysterious East. All over Europe, discoveries in medicine and science, new thinking in politics and religion, and unimaginable journeys to new worlds were making people rethink their lives; and new writing by scholars, poets and playwrights found words for these experiences.

If Shakespeare had never lived, we could still be astonished at the outpouring of wonderful works by Sidney, Spenser, Marlowe, Kyd, Ralegh, Bacon, Donne, Jonson and many more. It was a golden age for writing, and you can read – and watch – today such stories as that of Dr Faustus, the man who sold his soul to the devil, and Abigail in *The Jew of Malta* (both of these by Christopher Marlowe) who had to face the terrible rage of her father. The writers of the Renaissance took some familiar characters and many new ones, in age-old predicaments, and through the magic of their verse lifted them above their own lives to speak to us about our own, centuries afterwards, powerfully and clearly.

But Shakespeare did live, and he towered like a giant above them all. His stories are great ones, the range of his thinking is vast and his verse is matchless. This book invites you to get to know six of his plays. And if you could have hailed a boat that day in 1599, and were rowed towards the south bank where the new crop of theatres nestled alongside the dirty river, you would have seen the flag waving from the small hut of the Globe's roof; and perhaps Shakespeare himself, looking with satisfaction at this new home for his own company, the King's Men. To be there, at the two o'clock performance on that first day, would have been witnessing a moment in history!

Shakespeare's theatre

What do you expect if you go to the theatre or the cinema today? A roof over your head! Warmth; nice, comfortable seats; drinks and food in the interval; peace and quiet to get on with watching . . .

What if you had gone to a performance of one of Shakespeare's plays? If you weren't well-off, you'd get wet on a rainy day. You'd be standing, jostled by nut- and apple-sellers; you could weave your way, mid-performance, to buy ale or relieve yourself into a bucket at the back; you might chat to your neighbours and stop to hiss or cheer the actors. You could look up at those better-off with the benefit of a small roof arching over their seats, dry and a bit more comfortable than you – though still crammed and staring enviously at the noblemen and women who sat luxuriously above the stage in splendid isolation.

In many ways, the theatre was very different. Imagine: no lights to dim the stage, getting you ready for the play to begin. No silence settling as the curtain rose on wonderful scenery. Odd costumes as actors reached for whatever was to hand in the 'tiring house', their dressing-room; and no women at all! Boy actors took the parts of young girls and older men played the women, for not until long after Shakespeare's death was it thought proper for women to appear on stage.

You might have gone to see a play in a private house, or in the courtyard of an inn, but Shakespeare wrote most of his plays for public theatres. By 1642, London had nine theatres, all open to the sky and built rather like small

Roman amphitheatres, holding about 2,000 people. Nothing quite like them had been known since the days of the Roman Empire, and more than 200 years would have to pass before another city would have so many again in one time. You would go along at about two o'clock in the afternoon, and there was certain to be a performance unless it was a time for worship, or a time when there was an outbreak of the plague and everyone was too frightened to come out. The popular theatres such as The Curtain, The Rose and The Swan had to be built in the London suburbs, outside the strict supervision of the London government authorities, because too many people were causing trouble by fighting.

In 1599, Shakespeare and his actors raised the money to build the Globe Theatre, quite near to the others, and this became the home to Shakespeare's theatre company. Someone at the time said that he had heard 'much speech of this new playhouse, which is said to be the fairest that ever was in England'. Many of Shakespeare's plays began here, then in 1613 it was set on fire by a spark from a cannon during a performance of Shakespeare's play *Henry VIII*, and it was burnt to the ground. The actors, including Shakespeare himself, paid for it to be rebuilt. The new theatre lasted until 1642, when it was closed again, and it was pulled down in 1644. (And that is part of another story . . . you could try finding out about the Civil War and what the Puritans thought about entertainment; how the Hope Theatre went back to bear-baiting. You can still find Bear Gardens and Rose Alley today.)

There are only a few drawings of the theatres that survive from those times, and we can only guess at some of the details. Sometimes, however, there are tantalising clues. The contract for the Fortune Theatre of 1600 says that it should be a copy of the Globe; the writer even refers to a diagram that he is including. The diagram has never been found! But in 1989, something very exciting happened: the remains of both the Globe and Rose Theatres were discovered, though the Rose Theatre is now buried under a new office block. A new Globe Theatre has been built, 200 metres from the site of Shakespeare's Globe, by people who love Shakespeare's work and who were determined that you should see for yourself what his theatre may have looked like. Using green oak, lime and plaster, and bricks moulded to the same size as in Shakespeare's day, it is the first thatched building in central London since the Great Fire of 1666.

We know that in Shakespeare's Globe the main stage jutted out like a big platform into the unroofed 'yard' where many of the audience stood, and there was a trap-door through which actors playing ghosts and spirits rose and disappeared. There were no 'wings' (the sides of a modern stage from which actors come on today), but doors at the back. Most theatres had two or three levels for the actors to use, and one might be an 'inner stage' on top of a curtained 'discovery' space at the back of the main stage. Characters could hide there, or 'eavesdrop' on conversations taking place up front on the main stage. Musicians often played at the very top. A hut on the roof contained machinery for sound effects and various special effects such as the lowering and raising of a character playing a god. Three tiers of galleries enclosed the yard, and the Globe was probably round or hexagonal (six-sided).

So it was all very different from today. If you were taken back in a time machine, it would seem almost frighteningly different. The press of the crowd; the noise; the lack of safety regulations – what if you had been at the Globe on the night of the fire? Do you think you might have got out alive? But for Shakespeare's audiences, *this* was the theatre. They got by without complicated scenery and magical lighting, and his language gave the people their clues as to time and place. For example, when the Fairy King, Oberon, meets Queen Titania in *A Midsummer Night's Dream*, he says, 'Ill met by moonlight, proud Titania!' and he asks her, 'How long within this wood intend you stay?' Perhaps torches might be used to suggest the dark, and a table or a bed might be carried on if needed, but Shakespeare's words brought on the night, and painted the backdrops of castles and forests and wild heathland. When he wanted to menace you with the magic power of someone like Oberon, Titania could cry that the winds in revenge for his anger have 'sucked up from the sea contagious fogs' and the moon, 'the governess of floods, pale in her anger, washes all the air, that rheumatic diseases do abound'. The audience's imagination could get to work with such a description. In this important way, nothing has changed.

Shakespeare's plays

Plays in Shakespeare's day were not written down to be printed as books, but spoken and kept in people's memories. Someone would hold a 'prompt-book', a complete copy with detailed instructions for performing the play. Individual actors had the lines for their own parts. (They would make sure they knew the lines that came before them so that they could get ready to speak.) This collection of working scripts would come together again and again over several productions with some differences each time, and getting an accurate copy of the original would have been enormously difficult.

Today we have thirty-seven plays that we know were written by Shakespeare. It is tantalising to think that one or more may have been lost, and exciting to think that perhaps one day an old and dusty manuscript will turn up somewhere. But the fact that we have these thirty-seven at all is due to the devotion and hard work of two of Shakespeare's oldest friends. John Heminges and Henry Condell loved him so much, both as a writer and as a human being, that they spent seven years after his death gathering his plays into a single book. It was published in 1623, and it is now known as the First Folio. They wrote at the front of the book that they had collected his plays not for 'self-profit or fame, only to keep the memory of so worthy a friend and fellow alive'. They succeeded beyond their wildest dreams, for no one is more alive than William Shakespeare, who has given us the richest imaginary world ever created by a single man or woman.

The plays can be described under three headings: Comedy, Tragedy and History.

The comedies

A comedy is a play which has a thread of joy running all the way through it, and which ends happily for most of its characters.

The Comedy of Errors
Love's Labour's Lost
The Taming of the Shrew
The Two Gentlemen of Verona
A Midsummer Night's Dream
The Merchant of Venice
The Merry Wives of Windsor
As You Like It
Much Ado About Nothing
Twelfth Night
All's Well that Ends Well
Measure for Measure
The Winter's Tale
The Tempest
Pericles

The tragedies

A tragedy is a play in which the characters struggle despairingly with their lives before meeting with an untimely death.

Titus Andronicus
Romeo and Juliet
Julius Caesar
Hamlet
Troilus and Cressida
Othello

Macbeth
King Lear
Timon of Athens
Antony and Cleopatra
Coriolanus
Cymbeline

The histories

A history play tells the story of something that actually happened in the past.

King John
Richard II
Henry IV Part One
Henry IV Part Two
Henry V
Henry VI Part One
Henry VI Part Two
Henry VI Part Three
Richard III
Henry VIII

It is important to remember that the comedies often have moments of sadness, and that the tragedies contain some happiness, often making real events in history their starting point. The history plays are not meant to be accurate; there are some facts that Queen Elizabeth I would not have wanted to be acted out! Shakespeare was in any case more interested in a world of creation, and (with some caution) he used people and events as he liked.

Twelfth Night

About the play

The title refers to the ancient Festival of Fools, a time of carnival when everything is turned upside-down. The action takes place in an imaginary country called Illyria, and two groups of people are affected by the 'upside-downness' of the things that happen: the Countess Olivia and the Duke Orsino (who live in their grand houses, the Duke very much in love with Olivia), and the members of Olivia's household (her family, friends and the servants who look after her).

Into their lives burst Sebastian and Viola, a twin brother and sister who have been shipwrecked off the coast of Illyria. Viola dresses up as a boy and Olivia falls in love with her. There's more muddle when Sebastian finally turns up too and no one can tell the difference between them. Meanwhile, trouble develops between Olivia's steward, Malvolio (who runs Olivia's household), and everyone else who lives there. Like all of Shakespeare's comedies, everything gets sorted out in the end, and only poor Malvolio ends up feeling very sorry for himself.

About this scene

Characters

SIR TOBY BELCH, Olivia's uncle
SIR ANDREW AGUECHEEK, Sir Toby's friend
MALVOLIO, Olivia's steward
MARIA, Olivia's serving-woman
FABIAN, a servant

Everyone finds Malvolio very pompous and they decide to play a trick on him. They make up a letter which is all about how much Olivia loves him, sign it with her name and then leave it lying around. Then they quickly hide to watch him find it, certain of a good laugh at his expense. To their glee he walks straight into their trap. Even better! He's talking to himself, already imagining himself as her husband.

Act 2 Scene 5

Olivia's garden.

Enter SIR TOBY BELCH, SIR ANDREW AGUECHEEK, FABIAN and MARIA.

. . .

SIR TOBY

Here comes the little villain. How now, my metal 1
of India?

MARIA

Get ye all three into the box-tree. (*They hide behind the hedge*) Malvolio's coming down this walk; he has been yonder i' the sun, practising behaviour 5
to his own shadow this half hour. Observe him, for the love of mockery; for I know this letter will make a contemplative idiot of him. Close, in the name of jesting! Lie thou there; (*She throws down a letter*) for here comes the trout that must be 10
caught with tickling.

Exit

Enter MALVOLIO.

MALVOLIO

'T is but fortune; all is fortune. Maria once told me she did affect me; and I have heard herself

come thus near, that, should she fancy, it should
be one of my complexion. Besides, she uses me   15
with a more exalted respect than any one else that
follows her. What should I think on 't?

SIR TOBY (*To* SIR ANDREW and FABIAN)
Here's an overweening rogue!

FABIAN
O, peace! Contemplation makes a rare turkey-
cock of him; how he jets under his advanced   20
plumes!

SIR ANDREW
'Slight, I could so beat the rogue!

SIR TOBY
Peace! I say!

MALVOLIO
To be Count Malvolio!

SIR TOBY
Ah, rogue!   25

SIR ANDREW
Pistol him, pistol him.

SIR TOBY
Peace! peace!

MALVOLIO
There is example for 't; the lady of the Strachy
married the yeoman of the wardrobe.

SIR ANDREW
Fie on him, Jezebel!   30

FABIAN
O, peace! now he's deeply in; look how
imagination blows him.

MALVOLIO
Having been three months married to her, sitting
in my state, –

12

SIR TOBY

    O! for a stone-bow, to hit him in the eye.   35

MALVOLIO

    Calling my officers about me, in my branched velvet gown; having come from a day-bed, where I have left Olivia sleeping, –

SIR TOBY

    Fire and brimstone!

FABIAN

    O, peace! peace!   40

MALVOLIO

    And then to have the humour of state; and after a demure travel of regard, telling them I know my place, as I would they should do theirs, to ask for my kinsman Toby, –

SIR TOBY

    Bolts and shackles!   45

FABIAN

    O, peace, peace, peace! Now, now.

MALVOLIO

    Seven of my people, with an obedient start, make out for him. I frown the while, and perchance wind up my watch, or play with my – some rich jewel. Toby approaches, curtsies there to me, –   50

SIR TOBY

    Shall this fellow live?

FABIAN

    Though our silence be drawn from us with cars, yet peace!

MALVOLIO

    I extend my hand to him thus, quenching my familiar smile with an austere regard of control –   55

SIR TOBY

And does not Toby take you a blow o' the lips
then?

MALVOLIO

Saying, 'Cousin Toby, my fortunes having cast me
on your niece, give me this prerogative of speech,' –

SIR TOBY

What, what?   60

MALVOLIO

'You must amend your drunkenness.'

SIR TOBY

Out, scab!

FABIAN

Nay, patience, or we break the sinews of our plot.

MALVOLIO

'Besides, you waste the treasure of your time with
a foolish knight,' –   65

SIR ANDREW

That's me, I warrant you.

MALVOLIO

'One Sir Andrew,' –

SIR ANDREW

I knew 't was I; for many do call me fool.

MALVOLIO

(*Seeing the letter on the ground*) What employment
have we here?   70

FABIAN

Now is the woodcock near the gin.

SIR TOBY

O, peace! and the spirit of humours intimate
reading aloud to him!

14

MALVOLIO

(*Picking up the letter*) By my life, this is my lady's hand! These be her very *C*'s, her *U*'s, and her *T*'s; and thus makes she her great *P*'s. It is, in contempt of question, her hand.   75

SIR ANDREW

Her *C*'s, her *U*'s, and her *T*'s; why that?

MALVOLIO (*Reading*)

To the unknown beloved, this, and my good wishes: Her very phrases! By your leave, wax. (*He opens the letter*) Soft! and the impressure her Lucrece, with which she uses to seal; 't is my lady. To whom should this be?   80

FABIAN

This wins him, liver and all.

MALVOLIO (*Reading*)

> *Jove knows I love,*   85
> *But who?*
> *Lips, do not move.*
> *No man must know.*

'No man must know.' What follows? The number's altered!   90

'No man must know.' If this should be thee, Malvolio?

SIR TOBY

Marry, hang, thee, brock!

MALVOLIO (*Reading*)

> *I may command where I adore,*
> *But silence, like a Lucrece knife,*   95
> *With bloodless stroke my heart doth gore:*
> *M, O, A, I, doth sway my life.*

FABIAN

A fustian riddle!

SIR TOBY

Excellent wench, say I.

MALVOLIO

'*M, O, A, I,* doth sway my life.' Nay, but first, let me   100
see, let me see, let me see.

FABIAN

What a dish o' poison has she dressed him!

SIR TOBY

And with what wing the staniel checks at it!

MALVOLIO

'I may command where I adore.' Why, she may
command me; I serve her; she is my lady. Why, this   105
is evident to any formal capacity; there is no
obstruction in this. And the end, – What should
that alphabetical position portend? If I could
make that resemble something in me – Softly! *M,*
O, A, I, –   110

SIR TOBY

O! ay, make up that; he is now at a cold scent.

FABIAN

Sowter will cry upon 't, for all this, though it be as
rank as a fox.

MALVOLIO

M, Malvolio; *M,* why, that begins my name!

FABIAN

Did not I say he would work it out? the cur is   115
excellent at faults.

MALVOLIO

M, – but then there is no consonancy in the
sequel; that suffers under probation; *A* should
follow, but *O* does.

FABIAN

And *O* shall end, I hope.   120

SIR TOBY

Ay, or I'll cudgel him, and make him cry *O*!

MALVOLIO

And then *I* comes behind.

FABIAN

Ay, an you had any eye behind you, you might see
more detraction at your heels than fortunes
before you.   125

MALVOLIO

M, O, A, I; this simulation is not as the former; and
yet, to crush this a little, it would bow to me, for
every one of these letters are in my name. Soft!
here follows prose.

(*Reading*) *If this fall into thy hand, revolve! In my stars* 130
I am above thee; but be not afraid of greatness; some are
born great, some achieve greatness, and some have
greatness thrust upon them. Thy Fates open their hands;
let thy blood and spirit embrace them, and to inure
thyself to what thou art like to be, cast thy humble slough 135
and appear fresh. Be opposite with a kinsman, surly
with servants; let thy tongue tang arguments of state;
put thyself into the trick of singularity: she thus advises
thee that sighs for thee. Remember who commended thy
yellow stockings, and wished to see thee ever cross- 140
gartered; I say, remember. Go to, thou art made if thou
desirest to be so; if not, let me see thee a steward still, the
fellow of servants, and not worthy to touch Fortune's
fingers. Farewell. She that would alter services with thee,
                            THE FORTUNATE-UNHAPPY 145

Daylight and champain discovers not more; this is
open. I will be proud, I will read politic authors, I

will baffle Sir Toby, I will wash off gross acquaintance, I will be point-devise the very man. I do not now fool myself, to let imagination jade 150 me; for every reason excites to this, that my lady loves me. She did commend my yellow stockings of late; she did praise my leg being cross-gartered; and in this she manifests herself to my love, and with a kind of injunction drives me to these habits 155 of her liking. I thank my stars I am happy. I will be strange, stout, in yellow stockings, and cross-gartered, even with the swiftness of putting on. Jove and my stars be praised! Here is yet a postscript. 160

(*Reading*) *Thou canst not choose but know who I am. If thou entertainest my love, let it appear in thy smiling; thy smile becomes thee well; therefore in my presence still smile, dear my sweet, I prithee.*

Jove, I thank thee. I will smile; I will do every thing 165 that thou wilt have me.

Exit

FABIAN

I will not give my part of this sport for a pension of thousands to be paid from the Sophy.

SIR TOBY

I could marry this wench for this device.

SIR ANDREW

So could I too. 170

SIR TOBY

And ask no other dowry with her but such another jest.

SIR ANDREW

Nor I neither.

FABIAN

Here comes my noble gull-catcher.

Re-enter MARIA.

. . .

SIR TOBY

Why, thou hast put him in such a dream, that   175
when the image of it leaves him he must run mad.

MARIA

Nay, but say true; does it work upon him?

SIR TOBY

Like aqua-vitae with a midwife.

MARIA

If you will then see the fruits of the sport, mark his
first approach before my lady; he will come to her   180
in yellow stockings, and 't is a colour she abhors;
and cross-gartered, a fashion she detests; and he
will smile upon her, which will now be so
unsuitable to her disposition, being addicted to a
melancholy as she is, that it cannot but turn him   185
into a notable contempt. If you will see it, follow
me.

SIR TOBY

To the gates of Tartar, thou most excellent devil of
wit.

SIR ANDREW

I'll make one too.   190

                                      Exeunt

Julius Caesar

About the play

Julius Caesar is the ruler of Rome. Some of his senators fear that he has become too powerful and that this will not be good for the people. Led by Cassius, they decide that something has to be done. With the help of the noble Brutus they make a plan to kill him. On the morning of the Ides (the 15th) of March, 44 BC, they stab him to death. Mark Antony, Caesar's friend, can hardly believe it and he speaks to the people at Caesar's funeral, urging them to share his outrage and rise up against the conspirators.

Mark Antony leads a force into battle against the conspirators and defeats them at the Battle of Philippi. Brutus and Cassius kill themselves and Antony is left to mourn so many needless deaths, saying of Brutus, at the end of the play, these famous lines:

> This was the noblest Roman of them all.
> . . .
> His life was gentle, and the elements
> So mixed in him that nature might stand up,
> And say to all the world, 'This was a man!'

About these scenes

Characters

Act 2 Scene 1

BRUTUS
CASSIUS
CASCA
DECIUS   } senators of Rome
CINNA
METELLUS
TREBONIUS
LUCIUS, Brutus' servant

Act 2 Scene 2

CAESAR
CALPURNIA, Caesar's wife
SERVANT
DECIUS

Lucius discovers a letter and hands it to his master, Brutus.
Brutus quickly sees that a number of his friends are asking
him to join in a conspiracy against Caesar. He is a loyal
follower of Caesar, and deeply concerned that what they
want to do is wrong. At the same time he too is worried
about Caesar's growing ambition. He is finally persuaded that
Caesar must die and promises to join the conspirators. They
also have to face the fact that Mark Antony will oppose them
and they wonder if they should plan for his death too. Brutus
knows in his heart that they are wading through blood but
can see no alternative.

There is one practical problem: Caesar may not venture out
the next day because everyone knows that he is superstitious
and the night has been full of terrors. People are saying that
in the great storm that has raged through the Capitol, a lion
has walked the streets and graves have gaped open. Indeed,

21

in the morning, Calpurnia begs Caesar to stay at home,
fearing that these terrible things are portents, signs that he
should stay safe inside. Will he go?

Act 2 Scene 1

. . .

LUCIUS

 The taper burneth in your closet, sir:
 Searching the window for a flint, I found
 This paper, thus sealed up, and I am sure
 It did not lie there when I went to bed.

Gives him the letter.

BRUTUS

 Get you to bed again; it is not day.   5
 Is not tomorrow, boy, the Ides of March?

LUCIUS

 I know not, sir.

BRUTUS

 Look in the calendar, and bring me word.

LUCIUS

 I will, sir.

                                                     Exit

BRUTUS

 The exhalations whizzing in the air   10
 Give so much light that I may read by them.

Opens the letter, and reads.

 'Brutus, thou sleepst: awake, and see thyself:
 Shall Rome, &c. Speak, strike, redress.
 Brutus, thou sleepst: awake.'

. . .

'Shall Rome, &c.' Thus must I piece it out: 15
Shall Rome stand under one man's awe?

He begins to understand.

. . .

Re-enter LUCIUS.

LUCIUS
Sir, March is wasted fourteen days.

Knocking within.

BRUTUS
'T is good. Go to the gate. Somebody knocks:

Exit LUCIUS.

Since Cassius first did whet me against Caesar
I have not slept. 20

. . .

Re-enter LUCIUS.

LUCIUS
Sir, 't is your brother Cassius at the door,
Who doth desire to see you.

BRUTUS
Is he alone?

LUCIUS
No, sir, there are moe with him.

BRUTUS
Do you know them?

LUCIUS
No, sir; their hats are plucked about their ears,
And half their faces buried in their cloaks, 25
That by no means I may discover them
By any mark of favour.

BRUTUS
Let them enter:

Exit LUCIUS.

They are the faction. O conspiracy,
Sham'st thou to show thy dangerous brow by
   night
When evils are most free? O then, by day   30
Where wilt thou find a cavern dark enough
To mask thy monstrous visage?
  . . .

Enter the conspirators, CASSIUS, CASCA, DECIUS, CINNA,
METELLUS *and* TREBONIUS.

CASSIUS

   I think we are too bold upon your rest.
   Good morrow, Brutus. Do we trouble you?

BRUTUS

   I have been up this hour, awake all night.   35
   Know I these men, that come along with you?

CASSIUS

   Yes, every man of them; and no man here
   But honours you; and every one doth wish
   You had but that opinion of yourself,
   Which every noble Roman bears of you.   40
   This is Trebonius.

BRUTUS

                 He is welcome hither.

CASSIUS

   This, Decius Brutus.

BRUTUS

                 He is welcome too.

CASSIUS

   This, Casca; this, Cinna; and this, Metellus
     Cimber.

BRUTUS

They are all welcome.
What watchful cares do interpose themselves   45
Betwixt your eyes and night?

CASSIUS

                              Shall I entreat a word?

They whisper.

DECIUS

Here lies the east; doth not the day break here?

CASCA

No.

CINNA

O pardon, sir, it doth; and yon grey lines
That fret the clouds are messengers of day.   50

CASCA

You shall confess that you are both deceived:
Here, as I point my sword, the sun arises,
Which is a great way growing on the south,
Weighing the youthful season of the year; –
Some two months hence, up higher toward the
      north   55
He first presents his fire, – and the high east
Stands as the Capitol, directly here.

BRUTUS

Give me your hands all over, one by one.

CASSIUS

And let us swear our resolution.

      . . .

CASSIUS

But what of Cicero? Shall we sound him?   60
I think he will stand very strong with us.

CASCA

Let us not leave him out.

CINNA

No, by no means.

METELLUS

O let us have him, for his silver hairs
Will purchase us a good opinion,
And buy men's voices to commend our deeds.   65
It shall be said his judgement ruled our hands;
Our youths and wildness shall no whit appear,
But all be buried in his gravity.

BRUTUS

O name him not; let us not break with him,
For he will never follow any thing   70
  That other men begin.

CASSIUS

Then leave him out.

CASCA

Indeed, he is not fit.

DECIUS

Shall no man else be touched but only Caesar?

CASSIUS

Decius, well urged: I think it is not meet,
Mark Antony, so well beloved of Caesar,   75
Should outlive Caesar; we shall find of him
A shrewd contriver. And you know his means,
If he improve them, may well stretch so far
As to annoy us all, which to prevent,
Let Antony and Caesar fall together.   80

BRUTUS

Our course will seem too bloody, Caius Cassius,
To cut the head off, and then hack the limbs
Like wrath in death and envy afterwards,

For Antony is but a limb of Caesar.
Let us be sacrificers, but not butchers, Caius.   85
We all stand up against the spirit of Caesar,
And in the spirit of men there is no blood:
O that we then could come by Caesar's spirit,
And not dismember Caesar! But, alas,
Caesar must bleed for it. And, gentle friends,   90
Let's kill him boldly, but not wrathfully;
Let's carve him as a dish fit for the gods,
Now hew him as a carcass fit for hounds;
. . .
And for Mark Antony, think not of him;
For he can do no more than Caesar's arm   95
When Caesar's head is off.

CASSIUS
                                    Yet I fear him,
For in the ingrafted love he bears to Caesar –

BRUTUS
Alas, good Cassius, do not think of him.
If he love Caesar, all that he can do
Is to himself: take thought, and die for Caesar.   100
And that were much he should; for he is given
To sports, to wildness, and much company.

TREBONIUS
There is no fear in him; let him not die,
For he will live, and laugh at this hereafter.

Clock strikes.

BRUTUS
Peace, count the clock.

CASSIUS
                              The clock hath stricken three. 105

TREBONIUS
'T is time to part.

CASSIUS

But it is doubtful yet
Whether Caesar will come forth today or no;
For he is superstitious grown of late,
Quite from the main opinion he held once
Of fantasy, of dreams, and ceremonies.   110
It may be these apparent prodigies,
The unaccustomed terror of this night,
And the persuasion of his augurers,
May hold him from the Capitol today.

DECIUS

Never fear that. If he be so resolved,   115
I can o'ersway him; for he loves to hear
That unicorns may be betrayed with trees,
And bears with glasses, elephants with holes.
Lions with toils, and men with flatterers.
But, when I tell him he hates flatterers,   120
He says he does, being then most flatteréd.
Let me work;
For I can give his humour the true bent;
And I will bring him to the Capitol.

CASSIUS

Nay, we will all of us be there to fetch him.   125

BRUTUS

By the eighth hour; is that the uttermost?

CINNA

Be that the uttermost, and fail not then.

METELLUS

Caius Ligarius doth bear Caesar hard,
Who rated him for speaking well of Pompey;
I wonder none of you have thought of him.   130

BRUTUS

Now, good Metellus, go along by him;

He loves me well, and I have given him reasons;
Send him but hither, and I'll fashion him.

CASSIUS

The morning comes upon 's: We'll leave you,
    Brutus,
And, friends, disperse yourselves; but all
    remember   135
What you have said, and show yourselves true
    Romans.

BRUTUS

Good gentlemen, look fresh and merrily,
Let not our looks put on our purposes,
But bear it as our Roman actors do,
With untired spirits, and formal constancy;   140
And so, good morrow to you every one.

Exeunt all but BRUTUS.

Act 2 Scene 2

Thunder and lightning. Enter JULIUS CAESAR *in his night-gown.*

CAESAR

Nor heaven nor earth have been at peace
  tonight.
Thrice hath Calpurnia in her sleep cried out,
'Help, ho! They murder Caesar!' Who's within?

Enter a SERVANT.

SERVANT

My lord?

CAESAR

Go bid the priests do present sacrifice,   5
And bring me their opinions of success.

SERVANT

I will, my lord.

Exit

Enter CALPURNIA.

CALPURNIA

What mean you, Caesar? Think you to walk
  forth?
You shall not stir out of your house today.

CAESAR

Caesar shall forth; the things that threatened me,   10
Ne'er looked but on my back. When they shall
  see
The face of Caesar, they are vanishéd.

CALPURNIA

Caesar, I never stood on ceremonies,
Yet now they fright me. There is one within
Besides the things that we have heard and seen,   15

Recounts most horrid sights seen by the watch.
A lioness hath whelpéd in the streets,
And graves have yawned, and yielded up their
    dead;
Fierce fiery warriors fought upon the clouds
In ranks and squadrons and right form of war,   20
Which drizzled blood upon the Capitol.
The noise of battle hurtled in the air.
Horses did neigh, and dying men did groan,
And ghosts did shriek and squeal about the
    streets.
O Caesar, these things are beyond all use,   25
And I do fear them.

CAESAR
                  What can be avoided
Whose end is purposed by the mighty gods?
Yet Caesar shall go forth; for these predictions
Are to the world in general as to Caesar.

CALPURNIA
When beggars die, there are no comets seen,   30
The heavens themselves blaze forth the death of
    princes.

CAESAR
Cowards die many times before their deaths;
The valiant never taste of death but once.
Of all the wonders that I yet have heard,
It seems to me most strange that men should
    fear,   35
Seeing that death, a necessary end,
Will come when it will come.

Re-enter SERVANT.

What say the augurers?

SERVANT

   They would not have you to stir forth today.
   Plucking the entrails of an offering forth,   40
   They could not find a heart within the beast.

CAESAR

   The gods do this in shame of cowardice;
   Caesar should be a beast without a heart
   If he should stay at home today for fear.
   No, Caesar shall not. Danger knows full well   45
   That Caesar is more dangerous than he.
   We are two lions littered in one day,
   And I the elder and more terrible,
   And Caesar shall go forth.

CALPURNIA

                Alas, my lord,
   Your wisdom is consumed in confidence.   50
   Do not go forth today. Call it my fear
   That keeps you in the house and not your own.
   We'll send Mark Antony to the Senate house,
   And he shall say you are not well today.
   Let me, upon my knee, prevail in this.   55

CAESAR

   Mark Antony shall say I am not well,
   And, for thy humour, I will stay at home.

Enter DECIUS.

   Here's Decius Brutus; he shall tell them so.

DECIUS

   Caesar, all hail! Good morrow, worthy Caesar;
   I come to fetch you to the Senate house.   60

CAESAR

   And you are come in very happy time,
   To bear my greetings to the Senators,
   And tell them that I will not come today:

Cannot, is false: and that I dare not, falser:
I will not come today; tell them so, Decius.   65

CALPURNIA
Say he is sick.

CAESAR
                    Shall Caesar send a lie?
Have I in conquest stretched mine arm so far,
To be afeared to tell grey-beards the truth:
Decius, go tell them, Caesar will not come.

DECIUS
Most mighty Caesar, let me know some cause,   70
Lest I be laughed at when I tell them so.

CAESAR
The cause is in my will; I will not come.
That is enough to satisfy the Senate.
But for your private satisfaction,
Because I love you, I will let you know.   75
Calpurnia here, my wife, stays me at home:
She dreamt tonight she saw my statuë,
Which like a fountain with an hundred spouts
Did run pure blood, and many lusty Romans
Came smiling, and did bathe their hands in it;   80
And these does she apply for warnings and
    portents
And evils imminent; and on her knee
Hath begged that I will stay at home today.

DECIUS
This dream is all amiss interpreted.
It was a vision fair and fortunate.   85
Your statue spouting blood in many pipes,
In which so many smiling Romans bathed,
Signifies that from you great Rome shall suck
Reviving blood, and that great men shall press

For tinctures, stains, relics, and cognizance.   90
This by Calpurnia's dream is signified.

CAESAR

And this way have you well expounded it.

DECIUS

I have, when you have heard what I can say;
And know it now: the Senate have concluded
To give this day a crown to mighty Caesar.   95
If you shall send them word you will not come,
Their minds may change. Besides, it were a mock
Apt to be rendered, for some one to say
'Break up the Senate till another time,
When Caesar's wife shall meet with better
      dreams.'   100
If Caesar hide himself, shall they not whisper
'Lo, Caesar is afraid'?
Pardon me, Caesar, for my dear, dear love
To your proceeding bids me tell you this,
And reason to my love is liable.   105

CAESAR

How foolish do your fears seem now, Calpurnia!
I am ashaméd I did yield to them.
Give me my robe, for I will go.

Romeo and Juliet

About the play

This is the most famous love story in the world. Two teenage lovers are kept apart by their families who are locked into a bitter feud. They defy everyone and secretly marry. The friar who befriends them helps Romeo to run away and devises a plan by which shortly afterwards Juliet can join him. But it all goes terribly wrong. Romeo hears that Juliet has died and races desperately to be by her side in the family crypt. Seeing her, he kills himself with poison, for there is nothing left for him to live for. Juliet awakens from the friar's deceptive sleeping draught, ready to be with Romeo for the rest of her life, and in anguish sees his body. She kills herself with Romeo's dagger. When their two families find out, they are distraught. It is too late for the young lovers, but the Montagues and Capulets promise never to war with each other again.

About this scene

Characters

LORD CAPULET
COUSIN, to Capulet
TYBALT, Capulet's nephew
JULIET, Capulet's daughter
NURSE, to Juliet
SERVANT, in the Capulet household
ROMEO, Montague's son
BENVOLIO, Romeo's friend and Montague's nephew

This is where Romeo sees Juliet for the first time and falls in love. He has crept into a masked ball given by the Capulets, despite the danger of being recognised, and is looking for a girl he likes called Rosaline. Suddenly he sees Juliet and is instantly drawn to her beauty. Meanwhile Tybalt guesses who he is and furiously calls for his sword, intent upon fighting him. His uncle, for once, just wants peace and goodwill; who needs fighting when everyone is dancing and having fun? So Romeo and Juliet are free to meet, and they do.

Act 1 Scene 5

. . .

CAPULET

(*To his cousin*) Nay sit, nay sit, good cousin
    Capulet,
For you and I are past our dancing days.
How long is 't now since last yourself and I
Were in a mask?

COUSIN

By 'r Lady, thirty years.

CAPULET

What, man? 'T is not so much, 't is not so much: 5
'T is since the nuptial of Lucentio –
Come Pentecost as quickly as it will –
Some five and twenty years, and then we masked.

COUSIN

'T is more, 't is more; his son is elder, sir:
His son is thirty.

CAPULET

                   Will you tell me that?   10

  His son was but a ward two years ago.

  (*Observing the dancers*) Good youths i' faith, O
    youth's a jolly thing.

ROMEO

  (*To a servant*) What lady's that which doth enrich
    the hand of yonder knight?

SERVANT

  I know not, sir.   15

ROMEO

  (*To himself*) O she doth teach the torches to burn
    bright!

  It seems she hangs upon the cheek of night

  As a rich jewel in an Ethiop's ear;

  Beauty too rich for use, for earth too dear.

  So shows a snowy dove trooping with crows,   20

  As yonder lady o'er her fellows shows.

  The measure done, I'll watch her place of stand,

  And, touching hers, make blessèd my rude hand.

  Did my heart love till now? Forswear it, sight,

  For I ne'er saw true beauty till this night.   25

TYBALT

  This, by his voice, should be a Montague.

  Fetch me my rapier, boy. (*Exit page*) What dares
    the slave

  Come hither, covered with an antic face,

  To fleer and scorn at our solemnity?

  Now, by the stock and honour of my kin,   30

  To strike him dead, I hold it not a sin.

CAPULET

  Why, how now, kinsman! Wherefore storm you
    so?

TYBALT

Uncle, this is a Montague, our foe;
A villain that is hither come in spite,
To scorn at our solemnity this night.   35

CAPULET

Young Romeo is it?

TYBALT

                    'T is he, that villain, Romeo.

CAPULET

Content thee, gentle coz, let him alone;
'A bears him like a portly gentleman:
And to say truth, Verona brags of him
To be a virtuous and well-governed youth.   40
I would not, for the wealth of all this town,
Here in my house do him disparagement;
Therefore be patient, take no note of him.
It is my will, the which if thou respect,
Show a fair presence and put off these frowns,   45
An ill-beseeming semblance for a feast.

TYBALT

It fits when such a villain is a guest.
I'll not endure him.

CAPULET

                    He shall be endured.
What, goodman boy? I say he shall. Go to!
Am I the master here, or you? Go to!   50
You'll not endure him! God shall mend my soul,
You'll make a mutiny among my guests!
You will set cock-a-hoop! You'll be the man!

TYBALT

Why, uncle, 't is a shame.

CAPULET

                    Go to, go to!

You are a saucy boy. Is 't so indeed?   55
This trick may chance to scathe you, I know
    what.
You must contrary me! Marry, 't is time –
(*To the dancers*) Well said, my hearts! (*To* TYBALT)
    You are a princox; go
Be quiet, or – (*To the* SERVANTS) More light, more
    light, for shame! –
(*To* TYBALT) I'll make you quiet. – (*To the*
    dancers) What, cheerly, my hearts!   60

He leaves TYBALT *and moves among the guests.*

TYBALT
  (*To himself*) Patience perforce with wilful choler
      meeting,
  Makes my flesh tremble in their different
      greeting.
  I will withdraw, but this intrusion shall,
  Now seeming sweet, convert to bitterest gall.

                                          Exit

ROMEO
  (*Taking* JULIET's *hand*) If I profane with my
      unworthiest hand   65
  This holy shrine, the gentle sin is this:
  My lips, two blushing pilgrims, ready stand
  To smooth that rough touch with a tender kiss.

JULIET
  Good pilgrim, you do wrong your hand too
      much,
  Which mannerly devotion shows in this;   70
  For saints have hands that pilgrims' hands do
      touch,
  And palm to palm is holy palmers' kiss.

ROMEO

    Have not saints lips, and holy palmers too?

JULIET

    Ay, pilgrim, lips that they must use in prayer.

ROMEO

    O then, dear saint, let lips do what hands do: 75

    They pray, 'Grant thou, lest faith turn to despair.'

JULIET

    Saints do not move, though grant for prayers'

       sake.

ROMEO

    Then move not, while my prayer's effect I take.

    Thus from my lips, by thine, my sin is purged.

He kisses her.

JULIET

    Then have my lips the sin that they have took.   80

ROMEO

    Sin from my lips? O trespass sweetly urged!

    Give me my sin again.

He kisses her again.

JULIET

                  You kiss by the book.

NURSE *comes to* JULIET *from the side of the stage.*

NURSE

    Madam, your mother craves a word with you.

JULIET *joins her mother at the side of the stage.*

ROMEO

    What is her mother?

NURSE

                Marry, bachelor,

Her mother is the lady of the house,   85

And a good lady, and a wise and virtuous.

I nursed her daughter that you talked withal.

I tell you, he that can lay hold of her

Shall have the chinks.

ROMEO

              Is she a Capulet?

O dear account! My life is my foe's debt.   90

BENVOLIO

Away, be gone! The sport is at the best.

ROMEO

Ay, so I fear; the more is my unrest.

CAPULET

Nay, gentleman, prepare not to be gone:

We have a trifling foolish banquet towards.

The MASKERS *whisper their excuses to him.*

Is it e'en so? Why, then I thank you all.   95

I thank you, honest gentlemen; good night.

(*To the* SERVANTS) More torches here! Come on,

    then let's to bed.

              Torchbearers show the maskers out.

(*To himself*) Ah, sirrah, by my fay, it waxes late.

I'll to my rest.

           Exeunt all except JULIET *and* NURSE.

JULIET

Come hither, Nurse. What is yond gentleman?   100

NURSE

The son and heir of old Tiberio.

JULIET

What's he that now is going out of door?

NURSE

Marry, that I think be young Petruchio.

JULIET

What's he that follows there, that would not
   dance?

NURSE

I know not.   105

JULIET

Go ask his name (*Exit* NURSE) If he be marrièd,
My grave is like to be my wedding bed.

NURSE

(*Returning*) His name is Romeo, and a
   Montague,
The only son of your great enemy.

JULIET

(*To herself*) My only love sprung from my only
   hate!   110
Too early seen unknown, and known too late!
Prodigious birth of love it is to me,
That I must love a loathèd enemy.

NURSE

What's this, what's this?

JULIET

                    A rhyme I learnt even now.
Of one I danced withal.

JULIET's *mother calls her from another room.*

NURSE

                    Anon, anon!   115
Come let's away; the strangers all are gone.

                                        Exeunt

Macbeth

About the play

This is Shakespeare's most terrifying play. A great general, Macbeth, is on his way home after a battle. He is in the King of Scotland's army, and a good and loyal soldier. Suddenly three horrible witches appear, screeching at him. Frightened, he and his fellow-soldier Banquo hear astounding news: Macbeth will one day be king, and so will Banquo's children. The witches vanish, cackling, leaving the two men full of wonder and fear. But very quickly Macbeth becomes enthralled with the thought of being king and sets about doing anything that will help to make the prophecy come true. Murder follows murder as he loses his grip on all the values that had made his life good before; he stops being honest, just, fair, loyal . . . and instead becomes full of anger, hate and panic. His world darkens with evil and his end is a terrible one.

About this scene

Characters
THREE WITCHES
HECATE, the goddess of magic, ghosts and witchcraft
MACBETH
THREE APPARITIONS
LENOX, a nobleman

Macbeth goes back to see the witches. He is desperate to know if they can tell him more about the future. They conjure up some strange visions for him and he learns that for some reason another nobleman, Macduff, is a big threat to him. He also hears that no one who is born of a woman can hurt him, and that he will be safe until Birnam wood moves to Dunsinane. These last two predictions are hard to understand, but the first one is quite clear. Eight ghostly kings pass in front of him as well, and they all look like Banquo, a general who was once Macbeth's friend and whom Macbeth has already murdered. Does this mean that Banquo's children will inherit the crown and not his? Macbeth is clear about one thing: he's got to murder Macduff.

Act 4 Scene 1

A dark cave. In the middle, a boiling cauldron. Thunder. Enter the THREE WITCHES.

1 WITCH
Thrice the brinded cat hath mewed.

2 WITCH
Thrice, and once the hedge-pig whined.

3 WITCH
Harpier cries, 't is time, 't is time.

1 WITCH
Round about the cauldron go;
In the poisoned entrails throw.   5
Toad, that under cold stone
Days and nights has thirty-one
Sweltered venom, sleeping got,
Boil thou first i' th' charmèd pot.

ALL
Double, double, toil and trouble: 10
Fire, burn; and cauldron, bubble.

2 WITCH

Fillet of a fenny snake,
In the cauldron boil and bake;
Eye of newt, and toe of frog,
Wool of bat and tongue of dog,   15
Adder's fork, and blind-worm's sting,
Lizard's leg, and howlet's wing,
For a charm of powerful trouble,
Like a hell-broth boil and bubble.

ALL

Double, double, toil and trouble: 20
Fire, burn; and cauldron, bubble.

3 WITCH

Scale of dragon, tooth of wolf;
Witches' mummy: maw, and gulf,
Of the ravined salt-sea shark;
Root of hemlock, digged i' th' dark;   25
Liver of blaspheming Jew;
Gall of goat, and slips of yew
Slivered in the moon's eclipse;
Nose of Turk, and Tartar's lips;
Finger of birth-strangled babe,   30
Ditch-delivered by a drab,
Make the gruel thick and slab:
Add thereto a tiger's cauldron,
For th' ingredients of our cauldron.

ALL

Double, double, toil and trouble: 35
Fire, burn; and cauldron, bubble.

2 WITCH

Cool it with a baboon's blood:
Then the charm is firm and good.

Enter HECATE.

HECATE
> O, well done! I commend your pains,
> And every one shall share i' th' gains.   40
> And now about the cauldron sing,
> Like elves and fairies in a ring,
> Enchanting all that you put in.

Music and a song, 'Black spirits,' etc.

2 WITCH
> By the pricking of my thumbs,
> Something wicked this way comes. – (*Knocking*)   45
> Open, locks,
> Whoever knocks.

Enter MACBETH.

MACBETH
> How now, you secret, black and midnight hags!
> What is 't you do?

ALL
> A deed without a name.

MACBETH
> I conjure you, by that which you profess,   50
> Howe'er you come to know it, answer me:
> Though you untie the winds, and let them fight
> Against the churches, though the yesty waves
> Confound and swallow navigation up;
> Though bladed corn be lodged, and trees blown
>   down;   55
> Though castles topple on their warders' heads;
> Though palaces and pyramids do slope
> Their heads to their foundations; though the
>   treasure
> Of nature's germens tumble all together,

Even till destruction sicken, answer me   60
To what I ask you.

1 WITCH

          Speak.

2 WITCH

          Demand.

3 WITCH

          We'll answer.

1 WITCH

Say, if thou 'dst rather hear it from our mouths,
Or from our masters.

MACBETH

          Call 'em; let me see 'em.

1 WITCH

Pour in sow's blood, that hath eaten
Her nine farrow, grease, that's sweaten   65
From the murderer's gibbet, throw
Into the flame.

ALL

          Come, high or low,
Thyself, and office, deftly show.

Thunder. First APPARITION, *an armed head.*

MACBETH

Tell me, thou unknown power, –

1 WITCH

          He knows thy thought:
Hear his speech, but say thou nought.   70

1 APPARITION

Macbeth! Macbeth! Macbeth! beware Macduff;
Beware the Thane of Fife. – Dismiss me. –
   Enough.

          Descends

MACBETH

  Whate'er thou art, for thy good caution, thanks:
  Thou hast harped my fear aright. But one word
    more: –

1 WITCH

  He will not be commanded. Here's another,   75
  More potent than the first.

Thunder. Second APPARITION, *a bloody child.*

2 APPARITION

  Macbeth! Macbeth! Macbeth! –

MACBETH

  Had I three ears, I'd hear thee.

2 APPARITION

  Be bloody, bold and resolute: laugh to scorn
  The power of man, for none of woman born   80
  Shall harm Macbeth

                                                    Descends

MACBETH

  Then live, Macduff: what need I fear of thee?
  But yet I'll make assurance double sure,
  And take a bond of fate: thou shalt not live;
  That I may tell pale-hearted Fear it lies.   85
  And sleep in spite of thunder. –

Thunder. Third APPARITION, *a child crowned, with a
tree in his hand.*

                                         What is this,
  That rises like the issue of a king;
  And wears upon his baby brow the round
  And top of sovereignty?

ALL

                              Listen, but speak not to 't.

3 APPARITION

    Be lion-mettled, proud, and take no care   90
    Who chafes, who frets, or where conspirers are:
    Macbeth shall never vanquished be, until
    Great Birnam wood to high Dunsinane hill
    Shall come against him.

                         Descends

MACBETH

                That will never be:
    Who can impress the forest; bid the tree   95
    Unfix his earth-bound root? Sweet bodements!
      good!
    Rebellious dead, rise never, till the wood
    Of Birnam rise; and our high-placed Macbeth
    Shall live the lease of nature, pay his breath
    To time and mortal custom. – Yet my heart   100
    Throbs to know one thing: tell me (if your art
    Can tell so much), shall Banquo's issue ever
    Reign in this kingdom?

ALL

                Seek to know no more.

MACBETH

    I will be satisfied: deny me this,
    And an eternal curse fall on you! let me know. –   105
    Why sinks that cauldron? and what noise is this?

Hautboys.

1 WITCH
    Show!

2 WITCH
    Show!

3 WITCH
    Show!

ALL

    Show his eyes, and grieve his heart;   110
    Come like shadows, so depart.

A show of eight Kings, the last with a glass in his hand:

BANQUO's GHOST *following.*

MACBETH

    (*To the first King in his show*) Thou art too like the
      spirit of Banquo: down!
    Thy crown does sear mine eye-balls: (*To the second*
      King) and thy hair,
    Thou other gold-bound brow, is like the first: –
    (*To the* WITCHES) A third is like the former: –   115
      filthy hags!
    Why do you show me this? – a fourth? – Start,
      eyes!
    What! will the line stretch out to th' crack of
      doom.
    Another yet? – A seventh? – I'll see no more: –
    And yet the eighth appears, who bears a glass
    Which shows me many more; and some I see   120
    That two-fold balls and treble sceptres carry.
    Horrible sight! – Now, I see 't is true;
    For the blood-boltered Banquo smiles upon me,
    And points at them for his. – What! is this so?

1 WITCH

    Ay, Sir, all this is so: – but why   125
    Stands Macbeth thus amazèdly?
    Come, sisters, cheer we up his sprites,
    And show the best of our delights.
    I'll charm the air to give a sound,
    While you perform your antic round;   130
    That this great king may kindly say,
    Our duties did his welcome pay.

Music. The WITCHES *dance, and vanish with* HECATE.

MACBETH

Where are they? Gone? – Let this pernicious hour
Stand aye accursed in the calendar! –
Come in, without there!

Enter LENOX.

LENOX

What's your grace's will?   135

MACBETH

Saw you the weird sisters?

LENOX

No, my lord.

MACBETH

Came they not by you?

LENOX ·

No, indeed, my lord.

MACBETH

Infected be the air whereon they ride;
And damned all those that trust them! – I did hear
The galloping of horse: who was 't came by?   140

LENOX

'T is two or three, my lord, that bring you word,
Macduff is fled to England.

MACBETH

Fled to England?

LENOX

Ay, my good lord.

MACBETH

(*Aside*) Time, thou anticipat'st my dread exploits:
The flighty purpose never is o'ertook,   145
Unless the deed go with it. From this moment

The very firstlings of my heart shall be
The firstlings of my hand. And even now,
To crown my thoughts with acts, be it thought
    and done:
The castle of Macduff I will surprise, 150
Seize upon Fife; give to th' edge o' th' sword
His wife, his babes, and all unfortunate souls
That trace him in his line. No boasting, like a
    fool;
This deed I'll do, before this purpose cool:
But no more sights! – (*To* LENOX) Where are
    these gentlemen? 155
Come, bring me where they are.

                     Exeunt

A Midsummer Night's Dream

About the play

This is a story of a night of confusions in a haunted wood.
The passionate feelings of four young lovers are muddled up
by the mischievous magic of Puck, a spirit who can take any
shape and imitate any sound. Puck works for Oberon, King of
the Fairies. Oberon has quarrelled with his queen, Titania,
and the wood is alive with the presence of the fairies as the
lovers quarrel and lose their way, not realising that their
hopes and fears are being twisted and turned by magic. That
same night, six worthy workmen try to rehearse a play that
they want to perform in front of the Duke of Athens when he
gets married. They too get caught up in the magic.

When the night is over, everything returns to normal. Oberon
and Titania are reconciled, and the lovers are happily
matched and promised to each other as they wanted to be.
But one person – called Bottom! – is left with the curious
sensation that he has had a very strange dream.

About this scene

Characters
TITANIA
PUCK
FOUR FAIRIES

QUINCE
BOTTOM
SNUG
FLUTE   } the workmen
SNOUT
STARVELING

The workmen are gathered in a little clearing in the woods to rehearse their play. Bottom loves to take charge and the others find it difficult to get a word in edgeways. They are deeply involved when Puck turns up and is delighted to see who is there. Instantly he makes mischief and when Bottom exits and re-enters for his part, the poor man appears wearing an ass's head. What happens next, no one could have expected.

Act 3 Scene 1

The wood.

TITANIA *sleeps. Enter* QUINCE, SNUG, BOTTOM, FLUTE, SNOUT *and* STARVELING.

BOTTOM
   Are we all met?

QUINCE
   Pat, pat; and here's a marvellous convenient place for our rehearsal. This green plot shall be our stage, this hawthorn-brake our tiring-house; and we will do it in action, as we will do it before the   5
   Duke.

BOTTOM
   Peter Quince?

QUINCE

What sayest thou, bully Bottom?

BOTTOM

There are things in this comedy of Pyramus and
Thisby that will never please. First, Pyramus must   10
draw a sword to kill himself; which the ladies
cannot abide. How answer you that?

SNOUT

By 'r lakin, a parlous fear.

STARVELING

I believe we must leave the killing out, when all is
done.   15

BOTTOM

Not a whit; I have a device to make all well. Write
me a prologue, and let the prologue seem to say,
we will do no harm with our swords, and that
Pyramus is not killed indeed; and for the more
better assurance, tell them that I Pyramus am not   20
Pyramus, but Bottom the weaver; this will put
them out of fear.

QUINCE

Well, we will have such a prologue; and it shall be
written in eight and six.

BOTTOM

No, make it two more; let it be written in eight   25
and eight.

SNOUT

Will not the ladies be afeard of the lion?

STARVELING

I fear it, I promise you.

BOTTOM

Masters, you ought to consider with yourself, to
bring in, God shield us, a lion among ladies is a   30

most dreadful thing: for there is not a more
fearful wild fowl than your lion living; and we
ought to look to 't.

SNOUT

Therefore another prologue must tell he is not a
lion.   35

BOTTOM

Nay, you must name his name, and half his face
must be seen through the lion's neck; and he
himself must speak through, saying thus, or to the
same defect: 'Ladies', or 'Fair ladies' 'I would wish
you' or 'I would request you', or 'I would entreat   40
you, not to fear, not to tremble: my life for yours.
If you think I come hither as a lion, it were pity of
my life. No, I am no such thing; I am a man as
other men are'; and there indeed let him name his
name, and tell them plainly he is Snug the joiner.   45

QUINCE

Well, it shall be so: but there is two hard things,
that is, to bring the moonlight into a chamber;
for, you know, Pyramus and Thisby meet by
moonlight.

SNOUT

Doth the moon shine that night we play our play?   50

BOTTOM

A calendar, a calendar; look in the almanac; find
out moonshine, find out moonshine.

QUINCE

Yes, it doth shine that night.

BOTTOM

Why, then may you have a casement of the great
chamber window, where we play, open, and the   55
moon may shine in at the casement.

QUINCE

Ay, or else one must come in with a bush of thorns
and a lantern, and say he comes to disfigure, or to
present, the person of moonshine. Then there is
another thing; we must have a wall in the great   60
chamber; for Pyramus and Thisby, says the story,
did talk through the chink of a wall.

SNOUT

You can never bring in a wall. What say you,
Bottom?

BOTTOM

Some man or other must present Wall and let him   65
have some plaster, or some loam, or some
roughcast about him, to signify wall; or let him
hold his fingers thus; and through that cranny
shall Pyramus and Thisby whisper.

QUINCE

If that may be, then all is well. Come, sit down,   70
every mother's son, and rehearse your parts.
Pyramus, you begin; when you have spoken your
speech, enter into that brake; and so every one
according to his cue.

Enter PUCK *behind.*

PUCK

What hempen home-spuns have we swaggering   75
    here,
So near the cradle of the Fairy Queen?
What, a play toward? I'll be an auditor;
An actor too, perhaps, if I see cause.

QUINCE

Speak, Pyramus. Thisby, stand forth.

BOTTOM *as* PYRAMUS

Thisby, the flowers of odious savours sweet.   80

QUINCE

Odours, odours.

BOTTOM *as* PYRAMUS

Odours savours sweet;
So hath thy breath, my dearest Thisby dear.
But hark, a voice! stay thou but here a while,
And by and by I will to thee appear.   85

Exit behind

PUCK

A stranger Pyramus than e'er played here!

FLUTE

Must I speak now?

QUINCE

Ay, marry, must you; for you must understand, he
goes but to see a noise that he heard, and is to
come again.   90

FLUTE *as* THISBE

Most radiant Pyramus, most lily-white of hue,
Of colour like the red rose on triumphant brier,
Most brisky juvenal, and eke most lovely Jew,
As truest horse, that yet would never tire.
I'll meet thee, Pyramus, at Ninny's tomb.   95

QUINCE

Ninus' tomb, man! Why, you must not speak that
yet; that you answer to Pyramus: you speak all your
part at once, cues and all. Pyramus, enter: your
cue is past; it is 'never tire'.

FLUTE *as* THISBE

O, – As true as truest horse, that yet would never
tire.   100

Re-enter BOTTOM *wearing an ass's head.*

BOTTOM *as* PYRAMUS

If I were fair, Thisby, I were only thine.

QUINCE

O monstrous! O strange! We are haunted; pray, masters, fly! masters, help!

Exeunt all but BOTTOM *and* PUCK.

PUCK (*Coming forward*)

I'll follow you, I'll lead you about a round,
Through bog, through bush, though brake, through brier;   105
Sometime a house I'll be, sometime a hound,
A hog, a headless bear, sometime a fire;
And neigh, and bark, and grunt, and roar, and burn,
Like horse, hound, hog, bear, fire, at every turn.

Exit

BOTTOM

Why do they run away? This is a knavery of them   110
to make me afeard.

Re-enter SNOUT.

SNOUT

O Bottom, thou art changed! What do I see on thee?

BOTTOM

What do you see? You see an ass-head of your own, do you?   115

Exit SNOUT.

Re-enter QUINCE.

QUINCE

Bless thee Bottom, bless thee! thou art translated!

Exit

BOTTOM

I see their knavery: this is to make an ass of me, to
fright me, if they could; but I will not stir from this

place, do what they can. I will walk up and down
here, and I will sing, that they shall hear I am not 120
afraid. (*Sings*)

> The ousel cock, so black of hue,
> With orange-tawny bill,
> The throstle with his note so true,
> The wren with little quill. 125

TITANIA (*Awaking*)
What angel wakes me from my flowery bed?

BOTTOM (*Sings*)

> The finch, the sparrow, and the lark,
> The plain-song cuckoo grey;
> Whose note full many a man doth mark,
> And dares not answer 'nay'. 130

For indeed, who would set his wit to so foolish a
bird? Who would give a bird the lie, though he cry
'cuckoo' never so?

TITANIA
I pray thee, gentle mortal, sing again;
Mine ear is much enamoured of thy note; 135
So is mine eye enthrallèd to thy shape;
And thy fair virtue's force perforce doth move
    me
On the first view, to say, to swear I love thee.

BOTTOM
Methinks, mistress, you should have little reason
for that: and yet, to say the truth, reason and love 140
keep little company together nowadays. The more
the pity that some honest neighbours will not
make them friends. Nay, I can gleek upon
occasion.

TITANIA
Thou art as wise as thou art beautiful. 145

BOTTOM

Not so, neither; but if I had wit enough to get out of this wood, I have enough to serve mine own turn.

TITANIA

Out of this wood do not desire to go;
Thou shalt remain here, whether thou wilt or no. 150
I am a spirit of no common rate;
The summer still doth tend upon my state,
And I do love thee; therefore, go with me.
I'll give thee fairies to attend on thee;
And they shall fetch thee jewels from the deep, 155
And sing, while thou on pressed flowers dost
    sleep:
And I will purge thy mortal grossness so
That thou shalt like an airy spirit go.
Peaseblossom, Cobweb, Moth, and Mustardseed!

Enter Four Fairies.

FIRST FAIRY

Ready.

SECOND FAIRY

        And I.

THIRD FAIRY

            And I.

FOURTH FAIRY

                And I.

ALL

                    Where shall we go?   160

TITANIA

Be kind and courteous to this gentleman;
Hop in his walks, and gambol in his eyes;
Feed him with apricocks and dewberries,
With purple grapes, green figs, and mulberries;

The honey-bags steal from the humble-bees,   165
And for night-tapers crop their waxen thighs,
And light them at the fiery glow-worm's eyes,
To have my love to bed, and to arise;
And pluck the wings from painted butterflies
To fan the moonbeams from his sleeping eyes;   170
Nod to him, elves, and do him courtesies.

FIRST FAIRY
Hail, mortal!

SECOND FAIRY
    Hail!

THIRD FAIRY
    Hail!

FOURTH FAIRY
    Hail!

BOTTOM
I cry your worships mercy heartily; I beseech your
worship's name?

FIRST FAIRY
Cobweb.   175

BOTTOM
I shall desire you of more acquaintance, good
Master Cobweb: if I cut my finger, I shall make
bold with you. Your name, honest gentleman?

SECOND FAIRY
Peaseblossom.

BOTTOM
I pray you, commend me to Mistress Squash, your   180
mother, and to Master Peascod, your father. Good
Master Peaseblossom. I shall desire you of more
acquaintance too. Your name, I beseech you, sir?

THIRD FAIRY
　Mustardseed.

BOTTOM
　Good Master Mustardseed, I know your patience　185
　well: that same cowardly, giant-like ox-beef hath
　devoured many a gentleman of your house. I
　promise you, your kindred hath made my eyes
　water ere now. I desire you of more acquaintance,
　good Master Mustardseed.　　　　　　　　190

TITANIA
　Come, wait upon him, lead him to my bower.
　The moon, methinks, looks with a watery eye,
　And when she weeps, weeps every little flower,
　Lamenting some enforcéd chastity.
　Tie up my love's tongue, bring him silently.　195

　　　　　　　　　　　　　　Exeunt behind

The Merchant of Venice

About the play

Bassanio is desperate to win the love of Portia. She is rich and he is poor, so he asks his friend Antonio to lend him 300 ducats as it might give him a better chance of marrying her. Antonio has money tied up in business affairs abroad, but goes off to borrow some from a Jewish money-lender called Shylock. A deal is struck: he can have the money but with one strange and harsh condition . . . Antonio must pay it back on the exact day promised or give Shylock a pound of his flesh.

Antonio is filled with horror when news comes in that his ships have sunk and all his money is lost. Portia dresses up as a male lawyer and defends him in court against Shylock's immovable insistence on keeping to the bargain. Her maid Nerissa disguises herself as Portia's male clerk. Portia argues cleverly that Shylock is indeed entitled to his pound of flesh but that if he spills one drop of blood in getting it, his own life must be forfeited, for it is against the law to threaten anyone's life in the way that he has done. This is clearly impossible, and Shylock is furious that he cannot win. The play ends with the safe arrival of Antonio's ships.

About this scene

Characters

THE DUKE OF VENICE
PORTIA
SHYLOCK
ANTONIO
BASSANIO
GRATIANO, friend of Antonio
NERISSA, Portia's maid and wife of Gratiano

Shylock and Antonio are standing up in court and Portia is
ready to cross-examine them. She asks Shylock to be merciful
and Bassanio offers him twice as much and more if only he
will back down. Shylock refuses and waits calmly for the
verdict which he is sure will be in his favour.

Act 4 Scene 1

. . .

DUKE
    Antonio and old Shylock, both stand forth.

PORTIA
    Is your name Shylock?

SHYLOCK
              Shylock is my name.

PORTIA
    Of a strange nature is the suit you follow,
    Yet in such rule that the Venetian law
    Cannot impugn you as you do proceed.   5
    (To ANTONIO) You stand within his danger, do you
        not?

ANTONIO
  Ay, so he says.

PORTIA
            Do you confess the bond?

ANTONIO
  I do.

PORTIA
    Then must the Jew be merciful.

SHYLOCK
  On what compulsion must I? tell me that.

PORTIA
  The quality of mercy is not strained;   10
  It droppeth as the gentle rain from heaven
  Upon the place beneath; it is twice blest:
  It blesseth him that gives, and him that takes;
  'T is mightiest in the mightiest; it becomes
  The thronèd monarch better than his crown.   15
  His sceptre shows the force of temporal power,
  The attribute to awe and majesty,
  Wherein doth sit the dread and fear of kings;
  But mercy is above the sceptred sway;
  It is enthronèd in the hearts of kings;   20
  It is an attribute to God himself;
  And earthly power doth then show likest God's
  When mercy seasons justice. Therefore, Jew,
  Though justice be thy plea, consider this,
  That in the course of justice none of us   25
  Should see salvation; we do pray for mercy,
  And that same prayer doth teach us all to render
  The deeds of mercy. I have spoke thus much
  To mitigate the justice of thy plea,
  Which, if thou follow, this strict court of Venice   30
  Must needs give sentence 'gainst the merchant
    there.

SHYLOCK

  My deeds upon my head! I crave the law,
  The penalty and forfeit of my bond.

PORTIA

  Is he not able to discharge the money?

BASSANIO

  Yes, here I tender it for him in the court;   35
  Yea, twice the sum; if that will not suffice,
  I will be bound to pay it ten times o'er
  On forfeit of my hands, my head, my heart;
  If this will not suffice, it must appear
  That malice bears down truth. And I beseech you   40
  Wrest once the law to your authority;
  To do a great right, do a little wrong,
  And curb this cruel devil of his will.

PORTIA

  It must not be; there is no power in Venice
  Can alter a decree establishèd;   45
  'T will be recorded for a precedent,
  And many an error by the same example
  Will rush into the state. It cannot be.

SHYLOCK

  A Daniel come to judgement! yea, a Daniel!
  O wise young judge, how I do honour thee!   50

PORTIA

  I pray you let me look upon the bond.

SHYLOCK

  Here 't is, most reverend doctor, here it is.

PORTIA

  Shylock, there's thrice thy money offered thee.

SHYLOCK

  An oath, an oath, I have an oath in heaven. –
  Shall I lay perjury upon my soul?   55
  No, not for Venice.

PORTIA

      Why, this bond is forfeit,
 And lawfully by this the Jew may claim
 A pound of flesh, to be by him cut off
 Nearest the merchant's heart. (*To* SHYLOCK) Be
  merciful,
 Take thrice thy money; bid me tear the bond.   60

SHYLOCK

 When it is paid, according to the tenor.
 It doth appear you are a worthy judge,
 You know the law; your exposition
 Hath been most sound. I charge you by the law,
 Whereof you are a well-deserving pillar,   65
 Proceed to judgement; by my soul I swear,
 There is no power in the tongue of man
 To alter me. I stay here on my bond.

ANTONIO

 Most heartily I do beseech the court
 To give the judgement.

PORTIA

      Why then thus it is: 70
 You must prepare your bosom for his knife.

SHYLOCK

 O noble judge! O excellent young man!

PORTIA

 For the intent and purpose of the law
 Hath full relation to the penalty,
 Which here appeareth due upon the bond.   75

SHYLOCK

 'T is very true. O wise and upright judge,
 How much more elder art thou than thy looks!

PORTIA

 (*To* ANTONIO) Therefore, lay bare your bosom.

SHYLOCK

                                      Ay, his breast,
So says the bond, doth it not, noble judge?
'Nearest his heart', those are the very words.   80

PORTIA

It is so. Are there balance here to weigh
The flesh?

SHYLOCK

             I have them ready.

PORTIA

Have by some surgeon, Shylock, on your charge,
To stop his wounds, lest he do bleed to death.

SHYLOCK

Is it so nominated in the bond?   85

PORTIA

It is not so expressed, but what of that?
'T were good you do so much for charity.

SHYLOCK

I cannot find it; 't is not in the bond.

PORTIA

(*To* ANTONIO) You merchant, have you anything
    to say?

ANTONIO

But little. I am armed and well prepared.   90
Give me your hand, Bassanio; fare you well,
Grieve not that I am fall'n to this for you,
For herein Fortune shows herself more kind
Than is her custom. It is still her use
To let the wretched man outlive this wealth,   95
To view with hollow eye and wrinkled brow
An age of poverty: from which ling'ring penance
Of such misery doth she cut me off.
Commend me to your honourable wife;

Tell her the process of Antonio's end, 100
Say how I loved you, speak me fair in death;
And when the tale is told, bid her be judge
Whether Bassanio had not once a love;
Repent but you that you shall lose your friend
And he repents not that he pays your debt. 105
For if the Jew do cut but deep enough,
I'll pay it instantly, with all my heart.

BASSANIO

Antonio, I am married to a wife
Which is as dear to me as life itself,
But life itself, my wife, and all the world, 110
Are not with me esteemed above thy life.
I would lose all, ay, sacrifice them all
Here to this devil, to deliver you.

PORTIA

Your wife would give you little thanks for that
Is she were by to hear you make the offer. 115

GRATIANO

I have a wife who I protest I love –
I would she were in heaven, so she could
Entreat some power to change this currish Jew.

NERRISA

'T is well you offer it behind her back;
The wish would make else an unquiet house. 120

SHYLOCK (*Aside*)

These be the Christian husbands! I have a
     daughter –
Would any of the stock of Barabbas
Had been her husband, rather than a Christian.
(*Aloud*) We trifle time; I pray thee pursue
     sentence.

PORTIA

    A pound of that same merchant's flesh is thine;   125
    The court awards it, and the law doth give it.

SHYLOCK

    Most rightful judge!

PORTIA

    And you must cut this flesh from off his breast;
    The law allows it, and the court awards it.

SHYLOCK

    Most learned judge! A sentence! Come, prepare!   130

PORTIA

    Tarry a little; there is something else:
    This bond doth give thee here no jot of blood;
    The words expressly are 'a pound of flesh';
    Take then thy bond, take thou thy pound of flesh,
    But in the cutting it, if thou dost shed   135
    One drop of Christian blood, thy lands and goods
    Are (by the laws of Venice) confiscate
    Unto the state of Venice.

GRATIANO

                     O upright judge! –
    Mark, Jew – O learned judge!

SHYLOCK

    Is that the law?

PORTIA

               Thyself shalt see the act;   140
    For as thou urgest justice, be assured
    Thou shalt have justice more than thou desir'st.

GRATIANO

    O learned judge! – Mark, Jew, a learned judge!

SHYLOCK

    I take this offer then; pay the bond thrice,
    And let the Christian go.

BASSANIO

Here is the money.   145

PORTIA

Soft!
The Jew shall have all justice; soft, no haste!
He shall have nothing but the penalty.

GRATIANO

O Jew! an upright judge, a learned judge!

PORTIA

Therefore prepare thee to cut off the flesh;   150
Shed thou no blood, not cut thou less nor more
But just a pound of flesh. If thou tak'st more
Or less than a just pound, be it but so much
As makes it light or heavy in the substance
Or the division of the twentieth part   155
Of one poor scruple – nay, if the scale do turn
But in the estimation of a hair,
Thou diest, and all thy goods are confiscate.

GRATIANO

A second Daniel, A Daniel, Jew! –
Now, infidel, I have you on the hip.   160

PORTIA

Why doth the Jew pause? (*To* SHYLOCK) Take thy
    forfeiture.

SHYLOCK

Give me my principal, and let me go.

BASSANIO

I have it ready for thee; here it is.

PORTIA

He hath refused it in the open court;
He shall have merely justice and his bond.   165

GRATIANO

A Daniel still say I, a second Daniel!

I thank thee Jew for teaching me that word.

SHYLOCK

Shall I not have barely my principal?

PORTIA

Thou shalt have nothing but the forfeiture,
To be so taken at thy peril, Jew.   170

SHYLOCK

Why then, the devil give him good of it;
I'll stay no longer question.

PORTIA

                    Tarry, Jew;
The law hath yet another hold on you.
It is enacted in the laws of Venice,
If it be proved against an alien   175
That by direct or indirect attempts
He seek the life of any citizen,
The party 'gainst the which he doth contrive,
Shall seize one half his goods; the other half
Comes to the privy coffer of the state,   180
And the offender's life lies in the mercy
Of the Duke only, 'gainst all other voice.
In which predicament I say thou stand'st;
For it appears by manifest proceeding,
That indirectly, and directly too,   185
Thou hast contrived against the very life
Of the defendant; and thou hast incurred
The danger formerly by me rehearsed.
Down, therefore, and beg mercy of the duke.

GRATIANO

Beg that thou may'st have leave to hang thyself.   190
And yet, thy wealth being forfeit to the state,
Thou hast not left the value of a cord;
Therefore thou must be hanged at the state's
    charge.

DUKE

That thou shalt see the difference of our spirit,
I pardon thee thy life before thou ask it;   195
For half thy wealth, it is Antonio's,
The other half comes to the general state,
Which humbleness may drive unto a fine.

PORTIA

Ay, for the state, not for Antonio.

SHYLOCK

Nay, take my life and all, pardon not that.   200
You take my house when you do take the prop
That doth sustain my house; you take my life
When you do take the means whereby I live.

PORTIA

What mercy can you render him, Antonio?

GRATIANO

A halter gratis; nothing else, for God's sake!   205

ANTONIO

So please my lord the Duke and all the court
To quit the fine for one half of his goods,
I am content; so he will let me have
The other half in use, to render it
Upon his death unto the gentleman   210
That lately stole his daughter.
Two things provided more, – that for this favour
He presently become a Christian;
The other, that he do record a gift,
Here in the court, of all he dies possessed   215
Unto his son Lorenzo and his daughter.

DUKE

He shall do this, or else I do recant
The pardon that I late pronouncèd here.

PORTIA
Art thou contented, Jew? What dost thou say?

SHYLOCK
I am content.

PORTIA
                Clerk, draw a deed of gift.   220

SHYLOCK
I pray you give me leave to go from hence;
I am not well; send the deed after me,
And I will sign it.

DUKE
                Get thee gone, but do it.

GRATIANO
In christening shalt thou have two godfathers;
Had I been judge, thou shouldst have had ten
    more,   225
To bring thee to the gallows, not to the font.

                         Exit SHYLOCK.

Activities: the six scenes

Twelfth Night

1 When Malvolio struts about at the start of this scene, Sir Toby, Sir Andrew and Fabian are hopping mad. They can't believe his cheek. The trouble is, they daren't spring out of their hiding place to challenge him as that would spoil the trick; they have to sit there and take it. Imagine you are one of them and rewrite your character's lines in modern English, giving yourself the opportunity to show just how mad you are in the language that you would use. Work from Sir Toby's 'Here's an overweening rogue!' to the finding of the letter.

2 Do you see Malvolio as a silly but harmless dreamer, a self-important idiot, or as genuinely honest and dignified? Shakespeare has written Malvolio's lines so that you can interpret them in more than one way, and actors playing his part have sometimes made the audience laugh at his expense, or sneer at him for being so foolish, or feel very touched by his hopes. How would you play him? Explain your reasons.

3 The letter that Malvolio finds tells him to do a number of things to show that he has read and understood it. He must be grumpy with the servants, for example, and wear cross-gartered yellow stockings which Olivia is supposed to admire (but really can't stand!). Write your own letter in which you pretend to encourage a friend to feel that she or he is loved by someone, using up-to-date ideas.

76

Julius Caesar

1 Brutus is deeply uncertain about what to do when people first talk about killing Caesar. By nature he is loyal and law-abiding. Then he promises to join the conspirators; he shares their worry for the future if Caesar increases his power. With a partner, think about the following:

a) If he doesn't join the conspirators, what might their reaction be?

b) Is Brutus a brave man?

c) What else could he do?

d) How convinced do you think he is about his decision? Look carefully at the first scene again.

Now write Brutus' thoughts after everyone has gone.

2 Calpurnia tries to use her influence to persuade Caesar to stay at home. How persuasive is she?

a) Draw a line to make two columns and put these headings at the top, then gather your information:

Calpurnia's reasons for staying	Caesar's reasons for going

b) If you were a servant overhearing Caesar and Calpurnia talking, whose arguments would most convince you? Why? Write down your reasons.

3 Decius manages to persuade Caesar that it would be stupid to stay at home. Look back at the second scene where he does this, then write a single line that might have silently passed through his mind when he hears those fateful words: 'Give me my robe, for I will go.' Everyone in the class could read their line aloud.

Romeo and Juliet

1 Tybalt is ready to explode with anger. Imagine that Lord Capulet had failed to stop him from making trouble: what do you think would have happened next? Firstly find Tybalt's line: "'T is he, that villain, Romeo.' Then continue the scene in your own words.

2 The scene ends with Juliet's horror as she finds out who Romeo is. They can't turn the clock back . . . it's too late and they have met and fallen passionately in love. Write Juliet's thoughts as she goes to bed that night.

3 Write a story for today in which two teenagers are kept apart by their families.

Macbeth

1 Near the start of the play, when Macbeth first murdered someone, he was frightened. In this scene, committing murder is a simple matter: Macduff is a threat; he had better be killed. Then we see Macbeth's mind working very fast indeed . . . Macduff has fled? Then better kill his family!

Is it always easier to do something wrong when you have already done it once? Write a play or a story set in modern times in which someone slips into a life of crime after an initial difficulty, hardly realising that this has happened.

2 Macbeth is brave enough to stride across the wild heathland and enter a dark cave where the witches can be found. He dares to ask them about the future, and has to watch grisly ghosts pass by in front of him. Look at the following statements describing him in this scene:

- Macbeth is afraid.
- He is angry.
- He is steely sure about what he's going to do next.

Work with a friend to find evidence in the play showing that Macbeth is all three of these things. It might help you to copy down some lines and then explain them in your own words. Use the statements above as headings.

3 Imagine you are Lenox; you didn't see the witches, and you are staring at Macbeth. Write down your thoughts and then take turns in the class to read them out aloud.

A Midsummer Night's Dream

1 Quince is trying to direct the play and Bottom keeps interrupting him. Act out the first part of the scene, lines 1 to 74, from Bottom: 'Are we all met?' to Quince: '. . . according to his cue' showing how difficult Bottom makes the rehearsal, even though he means well. Think about these points:

- Do you think Bottom shouts?
- Does he wave his hands about?
- Does he jump up and down with excitement?
- Does he push in front of people?

and

- Are the others excited as well, or impatient, or uncertain and glad of help . . . ?

2 What do you think of Bottom?

a) When the others run away from him, Bottom says (lines 117 to 118), 'I see their knavery: this is to . . . fright me, if they could.' Is he really brave, or just trying to convince himself that he is? Read the lines through to yourself or a partner and see what you think.

b) He quickly settles into the idea of being loved by the Queen of the Fairies, hardly finding it extraordinary at all. Find the lines he speaks that show his acceptance of Titania's adoration, then work out how you would say them, showing whether or not it makes him very happy or just very smug!

c) Here are some words that might describe him:

over-confident   secretly shy   clever   simple
affectionate   bossy   pompous   comic
lonely   kind

Choose three or four of them and, using the text to back you up, write your own description of Bottom.

The Merchant of Venice

1 Earlier in the play we are told that Antonio looks down on Shylock for being Jewish. In this scene we see how angry Shylock is, how determined he is to stick to the bond. What part might Antonio's racism play in Shylock's determination? Does it explain him? Does it excuse him? Write down an imaginary conversation between yourself and Shylock in which you talk about why he wants something as horrible as a pound of flesh.

2 Do you think it was easy for Antonio to approach Shylock at the start of the play? What if you had to ask your own worst enemy for help? Write a short story in which you show how you felt before, during and after such an event, and the extent to which this may have altered your feelings about this person.

3 Imagine that you are a journalist covering the trial for a major newspaper. Write about what happens, making it as sensational as you can. You could design a whole front page for your coverage.

What happens next?

Twelfth Night

Do you think Malvolio is successful? Does he charm Olivia with his yellow stockings and his funny manners? Write the scene in which the two next meet.

Julius Caesar

We know the conspirators are successful. Do you think they are successful straight away? Does Caesar really go out that day, and does it all go to plan? Does anyone try to stop them when they raise their daggers? Imagine you are there among the crowd when Cassius and his friends draw close to Caesar. Describe afterwards what you saw to the members of your family when you get home that night. (What you say will depend a great deal on whether or not you were loyal to Caesar.)

Romeo and Juliet

Romeo and Juliet have fallen in love, but Juliet's parents have already chosen a husband for her: a man called Paris. What do you think they say when she tells them she won't marry Paris? Describe this scene.

Macbeth

Macbeth has found out that he is almost unstoppable. He can plan the deaths of a whole family. Do you think he carries them out? Does he get to Macduff himself? Are his plans strengthened by this new twist of cruelty? Write down what happens.

A Midsummer Night's Dream

Does Titania go on loving Bottom? Does he like it? Is the magic of their strange love ever lifted? Imagine you are one of the workmen, hiding in the trees: describe what you see.

The Merchant of Venice

Shakespeare doesn't tell us what happened next to Shylock. The last act of this play continues with events in the lives of the other characters, including the news that three of Antonio's ships have survived and he is therefore once again a wealthy man. Imagine that you are either Shylock or Antonio, looking back at this time in your life. Describe your thoughts and feelings in a letter to someone who knows you well.

Twelfth Night

What happens next – what Shakespeare wrote

Characters

OLIVIA
MARIA
MALVOLIO
SIR TOBY BELCH
FABIAN

Olivia is feeling sad because she loves someone who does not
seem to love her. She sends for Malvolio, as she often does,
and fully expects him to be his usual 'sad and civil' self. Maria
says he's coming, but he's in rather a strange state! We know
that Malvolio is responding to the letter.

Act 3 Scene 4

Olivia's garden.

Enter OLIVIA *and* MARIA.

OLIVIA

. . .

Where is Malvolio? He is sad and civil,
And suits well for a servant with my fortunes;
Where is Malvolio?

MARIA

He's coming, madam; but in very strange manner.
He is, sure, possessed, madam.   5

OLIVIA
Why, what's the matter? Does he rave?

MARIA
No, madam; he does nothing but smile; your
ladyship were best to have some guard about you
if he come, for sure the man is tainted in 's wits.

OLIVIA
Go call him hither.   10

Exit MARIA.

I am as mad as he,
If sad and merry madness equal be.

Re-enter MARIA *with* MALVOLIO.

How now, Malvolio!

MALVOLIO
Sweet lady, ho, ho.

OLIVIA
Smilest thou?   15
I sent for thee upon a sad occasion.

MALVOLIO
Sad, lady! I could be sad; this does make some
obstruction in the blood, this cross-gartering; but
what of that? If it please the eye of one, it is with
me as the very true sonnet is, 'Please one, and   20
please all'.

OLIVIA
Why, how dost thou, man? What is the matter with
thee?

MALVOLIO
Not black in my mind, though yellow in my legs.
It did come to his hands, and commands shall be   25
executed; I think we do know the sweet Roman
hand.

OLIVIA

Wilt thou go to bed, Malvolio?

MALVOLIO

To bed! ay, sweetheart, and I'll come to thee.

OLIVIA

God comfort thee! Why dost thou smile so, and 30
kiss thy hand so oft?

MARIA

How do you, Malvolio?

MALVOLIO

At your request! Yes, nightingales answer daws.

MARIA

Why appear you with this ridiculous boldness
before my lady? 35

MALVOLIO

'Be not afraid of greatness'; 't was well writ.

OLIVIA

What meanest thou by that, Malvolio?

MALVOLIO

'Some are born great,' –

OLIVIA

Ha!

MALVOLIO

'Some achieve greatness,' – 40

OLIVIA

What sayest thou?

MALVOLIO

'And some have greatness thrust upon them.'

OLIVIA

Heaven restore thee!

MALVOLIO

'Remember who commended thy yellow
stockings' –   45

OLIVIA

Thy yellow stockings!

MALVOLIO

'And wished to see thee cross-gartered.'

OLIVIA

Cross-gartered!

MALVOLIO

'Go to, thou art made, if thou desirest to be so;' –

OLIVIA

Am I made?   50

MALVOLIO

'If not, let me see thee a servant still.'

OLIVIA

Why, this is very midsummer madness.

. . .

Good Maria, let this fellow be looked to. Where's
my cousin Toby? Let some of my people have a
special care of him; I would not have him   55
miscarry for the half of my dowry.

Exeunt OLIVIA *and* MARIA.

MALVOLIO

O, ho! do you come near me now? No worse man
than Sir Toby to look to me! This concurs directly
with the letter; she sends him on purpose that I
may appear stubborn to him; for she incites me to   60
that in the letter. 'Cast thy humble slough,' says
she; 'be opposite with a kinsman, surly with
servants; let thy tongue tang with arguments of
state; put thyself into the trick of singularity'; and
consequently sets down the manner how: as, a sad   65

face, a reverend carriage, a slow tongue, in the habit of some sir of note, and so forth. I have limed her; but it is Jove's doing, and Jove make me thankful! And when she went away now, 'Let this fellow be looked to'; fellow! not Malvolio, not   70
after my degree, but fellow. Why, everything adheres together, that no dram of a scruple, no scruple of a scruple, no obstacle, no incredulous or unsafe circumstance – What can be said? Nothing that can be can come between me and   75
the full prospect of my hopes. Well, Jove, not I, is the doer of this, and he is to be thanked.

Re-enter MARIA, *with* SIR TOBY BELCH *and* FABIAN.

SIR TOBY

Which way is he, in the name of sanctity? If all the devils of hell be drawn in little, and Legion himself possessed him, yet I'll speak to him.   80

FABIAN

Here he is, here he is. (*To* MALVOLIO) How is 't with you, sir?

SIR TOBY

How is 't with you, man?

MALVOLIO

Go off; I discard you; let me enjoy my private; go off.   85

MARIA

Lo, how hollow the fiend speaks within him! Did not I tell you? Sir Toby, my lady prays you to have a care of him.

MALVOLIO

Ah ha! does she so?

SIR TOBY

    Go to, go to; peace! peace! We must deal gently   90
with him; let me alone. How do you, Malvolio?
How is 't with you? What, man! defy the devil;
consider, he's an enemy to mankind.

MALVOLIO

    Do you know what you say?

MARIA

    (*To* SIR TOBY *and* FABIAN) La you! an you speak ill   95
of the devil, how he takes it at heart. Pray God, he
be not bewitched!

FABIAN

    Carry his water to the wise woman.

MARIA

    Marry, and it shall be done tomorrow morning if
I live. My lady would not lose him for more than   100
I'll say.

MALVOLIO

    How now, mistress!

MARIA

    O Lord!

SIR TOBY

    Prithee, hold thy peace; this is not the way; do you
not see you move him? Let me alone with him.   105

FABIAN

    No way but gentleness; gently, gently; the fiend is
rough, and will not be roughly used.

SIR TOBY

    Why, how now, my bawcock! how dost thou,
chuck?

MALVOLIO

Sir! 110

. . .

MARIA

Get him to say his prayers, good Sir Toby; get him to pray.

MALVOLIO

My prayers, minx!

MARIA

No, I warrant you, he will not hear of godliness.

MALVOLIO

Go, hang yourselves all! You are idle, shallow 115 things; I am not of your element. You shall know more hereafter.

Exit

SIR TOBY

Is 't possible?

FABIAN

If this were played upon a stage now, I could condemn it as an improbable fiction. 120

SIR TOBY

His very genius hath taken the infection of the device, man.

MARIA

Nay, pursue him now, lest the device take air, and taint.

FABIAN

Why, we shall make him mad indeed. 125

MARIA

The house will be the quieter.

SIR TOBY

Come, we'll have him in a dark room, and bound.
My niece is already in the belief that he's mad; we
may carry it thus, for our pleasure and his
penance, till our very pastime, tired out of breath,   130
prompt us to have mercy on him; at which time
we will bring the device to the bar, and crown thee
for a finder of madmen.

1 Olivia thinks that Malvolio is saying and doing some very peculiar things! Take any three and explain why they would strike her as nonsensical.

2 Do you find Malvolio funny or pathetic or both when he is talking to Olivia? Explain why.

3 Malvolio feels very cross and mixed-up when the others set about him. Are they being fair? Is there any point at which you would call a halt to the teasing if you were one of the characters?

If your answer is 'yes', copy down the last lines of Shakespeare's that you would allow and then write some lines of your own finishing off the scene.

If your answer is 'no', write some concluding lines of your own at the end of the scene to show what you think of the fun.

Julius Caesar

What happens next – what Shakespeare wrote

Characters
BRUTUS
FOUR PLEBEIANS
ANTONY

Caesar is dead. Brutus and the conspirators are relieved – it is
over. But something else is already beginning . . . the people
are restive and want to know why Caesar was killed! Brutus
decides to speak to them. Bravely he encourages them to
listen to Mark Antony too, though he knows that Antony
mourns Caesar's death and would not have joined them in
the murder.

Act 3 Scene 2

Enter BRUTUS *and* CASSIUS, *with a crowd of* PLEBEIANS.
BRUTUS *goes into the pulpit.*

PLEBEIANS
    We will be satisfied; let us be satisfied.

BRUTUS
    Then follow me, and give me audience,
        friends.
    Cassius, go you into the other street,
    And part the numbers:
    Those that will hear me speak, let them stay
        here;   5

Those that will follow Cassius, go with him,
And public reasons shall be rendered
Of Caesar's death.

1 PLEBEIAN

                  I will hear Brutus speak.

2 PLEBEIAN

I will hear Cassius, and compare their reasons,
When severally we hear them rendered.   10

3 PLEBEIAN

The noble Brutus is ascended. Silence!

BRUTUS

Be patient till the last.
Romans, countrymen, and lovers, hear me for my
cause, and be silent, that you may hear. Believe me
for mine honour, and have respect to mine   15
honour, that you may believe. Censure me in your
wisdom, and awake your senses, that you may the
better judge. If there be any in this assembly, any
dear friend of Caesar's, to him I say, that Brutus'
love to Caesar was no less than his. If then, that   20
friend demand why Brutus rose against Caesar,
this is my answer: Not that I loved Caesar less, but
that I loved Rome more. Had you rather Caesar
were living, and die all slaves, than that Caesar
were dead, to live all free men? As Caesar loved   25
me, I weep for him; as he was fortunate, I rejoice
at it; as he was valiant, I honour him; but, as he
was ambitious, I slew him. There is tears for his
love; joy for his fortune: honour for his valour:
and death for his ambition. Who is here so base   30
that would be a bondman? If any, speak, for him
have I offended. Who is here so rude that would
not be a Roman? If any, speak, for him have I
offended. Who is here so vile that will not love his

country? If any, speak, for him have I offended. I   35
pause for a reply.

ALL

None, Brutus, none.

BRUTUS

Then none have I offended. I have done no more
to Caesar than you shall do to Brutus. The
question of his death is enrolled in the Capitol,   40
his glory not extenuated, wherein he was worthy,
nor his offences enforced, for which he suffered
death.

Enter MARK ANTONY, *with Caesar's body.*

Here comes his body, mourned by Mark Antony
who, though he had no hand in his death, shall   45
receive the benefit of his dying, a place in the
Commonwealth, – as which of you shall not? With
this I depart, – that, as I slew my best lover for the
good of Rome, I have the same dagger for myself,
when it shall please my country to need my death.   50

ALL

Live, Brutus, live, live!

1 PLEBEIAN

Bring him with triumph home unto his house.

2 PLEBEIAN

Give him a statue with his ancestors.

3 PLEBEIAN

Let him be Caesar!

4 PLEBEIAN

                    Caesar's better parts
Shall be crowned in Brutus.   55

1 PLEBEIAN

We'll bring him to his house
With shouts and clamours.

94

BRUTUS
My countrymen, –

2 PLEBEIAN
Peace! Silence! Brutus speaks.

1 PLEBEIAN
Peace, ho!

BRUTUS
Good countrymen, let me depart alone,   60
And, for my sake, stay here with Antony.
Do grace to Caesar's corpse, and grace his
    speech
Tending to Caesar's glories, which Mark Antony,
By our permission, is allowed to make.
I do entreat you, not a man depart   65
Save I alone, till Antony have spoke.

Exit

1 PLEBEIAN
Stay, ho, and let us hear Mark Antony!

3 PLEBEIAN
Let him go up into the public chair.
We'll hear him. Noble Antony, go up.

ANTONY
For Brutus' sake I am beholding to you.   70

Goes into the pulpit.

1 There is an ominous start to this scene. The Plebeians say, 'We will be satisfied.' They are demanding an account of the conspirators' actions. You can feel the murmurs growing. What might you overhear individuals saying as you moved among them?

2 Brutus persuades them. How does he do it? Look at his speech, 'Be patient till the last' (lines 12 to 36). Rewrite this in modern English, then list his main arguments. Would he persuade you?

3 This crowd is dangerous.

a) How can you tell, as the scene develops, that the crowd has a will of its own?

b) How would you feel if you were Brutus, descending from the pulpit just as Mark Antony is preparing to go up into it?

c) What do you think Antony will try to say, and do you think he will be successful? (When you have talked about this find a copy of the play and look at Act 3 Scene 2, or turn to page 132 in this volume for one of his speeches.)

Romeo and Juliet

What happens next – what Shakespeare wrote

Characters

JULIET
LADY CAPULET
LORD CAPULET
NURSE

Romeo and Juliet are secretly married. Then, to her horror, Juliet's parents tell her that they have set a date for her to marry Paris. The household is already in uproar, for Tybalt has been killed by Romeo. Tybalt had killed Romeo's kinsman, Mercutio, and in rage and sorrow Romeo had gone after him. Juliet is pretending to hate Romeo for what he has done but in her heart she is yearning for the time when she will see him again and very fearful for their future. Bravely, she stands up to her parents.

Act 3 Scene 5

(*Lady Capulet is talking about Tybalt's death.*)

LADY CAPULET
  We will have vengeance for it, fear thou not.
  Then weep no more. I'll send to one in Mantua,
  Where that same banished runagate doth live,
  Shall give him such an unaccustomed dram

That he shall soon keep Tybalt company;   5
And then I hope thou wilt be satisfied.

JULIET

Indeed, I never shall be satisfied
With Romeo till I behold him; dead
Is my poor heart, so for a kinsman vexed.
Madam, if you could find out but a man   10
To bear a poison, I would temper it
That Romeo should upon receipt thereof
Soon sleep in quiet. O how my heart abhors
To hear him named and cannot come to him
To wreak the love I bore my cousin   15
Upon his body that hath slaughtered him.

LADY CAPULET

Find thou the means, and I'll find such a man.
But now I'll tell thee joyful tidings, girl.

JULIET

And joy comes well in such a needy time.
What are they, beseech your ladyship?   20

LADY CAPULET

Well, well, thou hast a careful father, child;
One who, to put thee from thy heaviness,
Hath sorted out a sudden day of joy
That thou expects not, nor I looked not for.

JULIET

Madam, in happy time! What day is that?   25

LADY CAPULET

Marry, my child, early next Thursday morn,
The gallant, young, and noble gentleman,
The County Paris, at Saint Peter's Church,
Shall happily make thee there a joyful bride.

JULIET

Now, by Saint Peter's Church, and Peter too,   30

He shall not make me there a joyful bride.
I wonder at this haste, that I must wed
Ere he that should be my husband comes to woo.
I pray you tell my lord and father, madam,
I will not marry yet; and when I do, I swear   35
It shall be Romeo, whom you know I hate,
Rather than Paris. These are news indeed!

LADY CAPULET
Here comes your father; tell him so yourself,
And see how he will take it at your hands.

Enter CAPULET *and* NURSE.

CAPULET
When the sun sets, the earth doth drizzle dew;   40
But for the sunset of my brother's son
It rains downright.
How now, a conduit, girl? What, still in tears?
Evermore showering? In one little body
Thou counterfeits a bark, a sea, a wind;   45
For still thy eyes, which I may call the sea,
Do ebb and flow with tears; the bark thy body is,
Sailing in this salt flood; the winds thy sighs,
Who raging with thy tears, and they with them,
Without a sudden calm will overset   50
Thy tempest-tossèd body. How now, wife?
Have you delivered to her our decree?

LADY CAPULET
Ay, sir, but she will none, she gives you thanks.
I would the fool were married to her grave!

CAPULET
Soft, take me with you, take me with you, wife.   55
How will she none? Doth she not give us thanks?
Is she not proud? Doth she not count her blest,
Unworthy as she is, that we have wrought
So worthy a gentleman to be her bride?

JULIET

Not proud you have, but thankful that you have. 60
Proud can I never be of what I hate,
But thankful even for hate that is meant love.

CAPULET

How, how! how, how, chop-logic! What is this?
'Proud', and 'I thank you', and 'I thank you not',
And yet 'Not proud', mistress minion you? 65
Thank me no thankings, nor proud me no
     prouds,
But fettle your fine joints 'gainst Thursday next,
To go with Paris to Saint Peter's Church,
Or I will drag thee on a hurdle thither.
Out, you green-sickness carrion! out, you
     baggage! 70
You tallow-face.

LADY CAPULET

(*To her husband*) Fie, fie! What, are you mad?

JULIET

Good father, I beseech you on my knees,
Hear me with patience but to speak a word.

CAPULET

Hang thee, young baggage! disobedient wretch!
I tell thee what: get thee to church o' Thursday, 75
Or never after look me in the face.
Speak not, reply not, do not answer me.
My fingers itch. Wife, we scarce thought us blest
That God had lent us but this only child,
But now I see this one is one too much, 80
And that we have a curse in having her.
Out on her, hilding!

NURSE

                    God in heaven bless her!
You are to blame, my lord, to rate her so.

CAPULET
And why, my Lady Wisdom! Hold your tongue,
Good Prudence. Smatter with your gossips, go.   85

NURSE
I speak no treason.

CAPULET
                    O God gi' good e'en!

NURSE
May not one speak?

CAPULET
                    Peace, you mumbling fool!
Utter your gravity o'er a gossip's bowl,
For here we need it not.

LADY CAPULET
                    You are too hot.

CAPULET
God's bread! it makes me mad.   90
Day, night, hour, tide, time, work, play,
Alone, in company, still my care hath been
To have her matched; and having now provided
A gentleman of noble parentage,
Of fair demesnes, youthful and nobly trained,   95
Stuffed, as they say, with honourable parts,
Proportioned as one's thought would wish a
    man,
And then to have a wretched puling fool,
A whining mammet, in her fortune's tender,
To answer 'I'll not wed, I cannot love,   100
I am too young, I pray you pardon me'!
But and you will not wed I'll pardon you:
Graze where you will, you shall not house with
    me.

Look to 't, think on 't; I do not use to jest.
Thursday is near; lay hand on heart, advise.   105
And you be mine, I'll give you to my friend:
And you be not, hang, beg, starve, die in the
   streets,
For, by my soul, I'll ne'er acknowledge thee,
Nor what is mine shall never do thee good.
Trust to 't, bethink you; I'll not be forsworn.   110

Exit CAPULET.

JULIET

Is there no pity sitting in the clouds
That sees into the bottom of my grief?
O sweet my mother, cast me not away!
Delay this marriage for a month, a week;
Or, if you do not, make a bridal bed   115
In that dim monument where Tybalt lies.

LADY CAPULET

Talk not to me, for I'll not speak a word.
Do as thou wilt, for I have done with thee.

Exit LADY CAPULET.

JULIET

O God! O Nurse, how shall this be prevented?

1 Lord and Lady Capulet are amazed at Juliet's reaction.
What did they expect, and why are they so angry? Look at
the situation from their point of view and write an
explanation for the strength of their feelings.

2 Juliet turns to her nurse for comfort, protection and
advice. What do you think would happen if she tried
approaching her mother again? Write this scene.

Macbeth

What happens next – what Shakespeare wrote

Characters

Act 4 Scene 2
LADY MACDUFF
SON
MESSENGER
MURDERER

Act 4 Scene 3
MACDUFF
ROSSE
MALCOLM, the son of the dead King of Scotland

Lady Macduff is at home and talking to her little son when a grim-faced but kindly messenger arrives. No sooner has he spoken than the murderers arrive.

Afterwards, Macduff, safely in England, greets his cousin Rosse hot from Scotland and hears the dreadful news.

Act 4 Scene 2

. . .

LADY MACDUFF
    (*To her son*) Poor prattler, how thou talk'st!

Enter a MESSENGER.

MESSENGER

Bless you, fair dame! I am not to you known,
Though in your state of honour I am perfect.
I doubt, some danger does approach you nearly:
If you will take a homely man's advice,   5
Be not found here; hence, with your little ones.
To fright you thus, methinks, I am too savage;
To do worse to you were fell cruelty,
Which is too nigh your person. Heaven preserve
    you!
I dare abide no longer.

Exit

LADY MACDUFF

                          Whither should I fly?   10
I have done no harm. But I remember now
I am in this earthly world, where to do harm
Is often laudable, to do good sometime
Accounted dangerous folly: why then, alas,
Do I put up that womanly defence,   15
To say, I have done no harm? What are these
    faces?

Enter MURDERERS.

MURDERER

Where is your husband?

LADY MACDUFF

I hope, in no place so unsanctified,
Where such as thou may'st find him.

MURDERER

                          He's a traitor.

SON

Thou liest, thou shag-haired villain!

MURDERER

                          What, you egg!   20

Stabbing him.

Young fry of treachery!

SON

He has killed me, mother:

Run away, I pray you!

Dies

Exit LADY MACDUFF, *crying 'Murder!' and pursued by the* MURDERERS.

Act 4 Scene 3 ·

England. A room in the King's palace.

Enter MALCOLM *and* MACDUFF.

MALCOLM

Let us seek out some desolate shade, and there
Weep our sad bosoms empty.

MACDUFF

Let us rather
Hold fast the mortal sword, and like good men
Bestride our down-fall birthdom. Each new morn,
New widows howl, new orphans cry; new sorrows   5
Strike heaven on the face, that it resounds
Which often, since my here-remain in England,
I have seen him do. How he solicits heaven,
Himself best knows; but strangely-visited people,
All swoln and ulcerous, pitiful to the eye,   10
The mere despair of surgery, he cures;
Hanging a golden stamp about their necks,
Put on with holy prayers: and 't is spoken,
To the succeeding royalty he leaves

The healing benediction. With this strange virtue   15
He hath a heavenly gift of prophecy;
And sundry blessings hang about his throne
That speak him full of grace.

Enter ROSSE.

MACDUFF

                           See, who comes here.

MALCOLM

My countryman; but yet I know him not.

MACDUFF

My ever-gentle cousin, welcome hither.   20

MALCOLM

I know him now. Good God betimes remove
The means that makes us strangers!

ROSSE

                                  Sir, amen.

MACDUFF

Stands Scotland where it did?

ROSSE

                         Alas, poor country!
Almost afraid to know itself. It cannot
Be called our mother, but our grave; where
    nothing,   25
But who knows nothing, is once seen to smile;
Where sighs, and groans, and shrieks that rend
    the air
Are made, not marked; where violent sorrow
    seems
A modern ecstasy: the dead man's knell
Is there scarce asked for who; and good men's
    lives   30
Expire before the flowers in their caps,
Dying or ere they sicken.

MACDUFF
                        O relation
  Too nice and yet too true!

MALCOLM
                        What's the newest grief?

ROSSE
  That of an hour's age doth hiss the speaker;
  Each minute teems a new one.

MACDUFF
                      How does my wife?   35

ROSSE
  Why, well.

MACDUFF
          And all my children?

ROSSE
                  Well, too.

MACDUFF
  The tyrant has not battered at their peace?

ROSSE
  No; they were well at peace when I did leave 'em.

MACDUFF
  Be not a niggard of your speech: how goes 't?

ROSSE
  When I came hither to transport the tidings,
  Which I have heavily borne, there ran a rumour   40
  Of many worthy fellows that were out;
  Which was, to my belief, witnessed the rather,
  For that I saw the tyrant's power afoot.
  Now is the time of help. Your eye in Scotland
  Would create soldiers, make our women fight   45
  To doff their dire distresses.

MALCOLM

                    Be 't their comfort,
We are coming thither. Gracious England hath
Lent us good Siward, and ten thousand men;
An older and a better soldier none   50
That Christendom give out.

ROSSE

                    Would I could answer
This comfort with the like! But I have words
That would be howled out in the desert air,
Where hearing should not latch them.

MACDUFF

                    What concern they?
The general cause? or is it a fee-grief   55
Due to some single breast?

ROSSE

                  No mind that's honest
But in it shares some woe, though the main part
Pertains to you alone.

MACDUFF

            If it be mine,
Keep it not from me; quickly let me have it.

ROSSE

Let not your ears despise my tongue for ever,   60
Which shall possess them with the heaviest sound
That ever yet they heard.

MACDUFF

           Humph! I guess at it.

ROSSE

Your castle is surprised; your wife and babes
Savagely slaughtered: to relate the manner
Were, on the quarry of these murdered deer,   65
To add the death of you.

MALCOLM
> Merciful heaven! –

What, man! ne'er pull your hat upon your brows:
Give sorrow words; the grief that does not speak
Whispers the o'er-fraught heart, and bids it
   break.

MACDUFF
My children too?

ROSSE
> Wife, children, servants, all   70

That could be found.

MACDUFF
> And I must be from thence!

My wife killed too?

ROSSE
> I have said.

MALCOLM
> Be comforted:

Let's make us medicines of our great revenge,
To cure this deadly grief.

MACDUFF
He has no children. – All my pretty ones?   75
Did you say all? – O hell-kite! – All?
What, all my pretty chickens, and their dam,
At one fell swoop?

MALCOLM
> Dispute it like a man.

MACDUFF
> I shall do so;

But I must also feel it as a man:
I cannot but remember such things were,   80
That were most precious to me. – Did heaven
   look on,

And would not take their part? Sinful Macduff!
They were all struck for thee. Naught that I am,
Not for their own demerits, but for mine
Fell slaughter on their souls: heaven rest them
    now!   85

MALCOLM

Be this the whetstone of your sword: let grief
Convert to anger; blunt not the heart, enrage it.

MACDUFF

O! I could play the woman with mine eyes,
And braggart with my tongue, – But, gentle
    heavens,
Cut short all intermission; front to front   90
Bring thou this fiend of Scotland and myself;
Within my sword's length set him; if he 'scape,
Heaven forgive him too!

MALCOLM

                    This time goes manly,
Come, go we to the King: our power is ready;
Our lack is nothing but our leave. Macbeth   95
Is ripe for shaking, and the powers above
Put on their instruments. Receive what cheer you
    may;
The night is long that never finds the day.

                          Exeunt

1 Lady Macduff's little son is very brave. What would you have done in his place?

2 Rosse finds it painfully difficult to disclose the news. Look at line 38: 'they were well at peace when I did leave 'em'. It is ambiguous: that is, he tries to put off the fateful moment by saying something that could be taken in two ways – one of which is that they were peacefully going about their ordinary business. He may have caught in Macduff's eyes the understanding that Rosse means the peace that comes with death, and is afraid to say so clearly. Write down the thoughts that Rosse might have had before speaking.

3 Macduff feels grief and rage, and Malcolm urges him to let his anger carry him forward so that he can defeat Macbeth all the more quickly. Imagine that you are Macduff, and that it is years afterwards: describe your powerful memories of that day.

A Midsummer Night's Dream

What happens next – what Shakespeare wrote

Characters

TITANIA
PEASEBLOSSOM
COBWEB } Titania's fairies
MUSTARDSEED
BOTTOM
OBERON
PUCK

Oberon watches Titania and Bottom in a woodland clearing.
The unlikely couple are very happy, attended by Titania's
fairies. Bottom is especially content, for he has never been
loved like this before! Oberon begins to repent, especially as
the reason for his action – the quarrel they had had over who
should have a little changeling boy for a servant – has now
been settled (Titania has given the child to him). Once again
Oberon gets ready to use his magic powers.

Act 4 Scene 1

The wood.

Enter TITANIA *and* BOTTOM, *with the fairies attending,
and* OBERON *behind, unseen.*

TITANIA

Come, sit thee down upon this flowery bed,

While I thy amiable cheeks do coy,
And stick musk-roses in thy sleek smooth head,
And kiss thy fair large ears, my gentle joy.

BOTTOM
Where's Peaseblossom?   5

PEASEBLOSSOM
Ready.

BOTTOM
Scratch my head, Peaseblossom. Where's
Monsieur Cobweb?

COBWEB
Ready.

BOTTOM
Monsieur Cobweb, good monsieur, get you your   10
weapons in your hand, and kill me a red-hipped
humble-bee on the top of a thistle; and good
monsieur, bring me the honey-bag. Do not fret
yourself too much in the action, monsieur; and
good monsieur, have a care the honey-bag break   15
not; I would be loth to have you overflown with
a honey-bag, signior. Where's Monsieur
Mustardseed?

MUSTARDSEED
Ready.

BOTTOM
Give me your neaf, Monsieur Mustardseed. Pray   20
you, leave your curtsy, good monsieur.

MUSTARDSEED
What's your will?

BOTTOM
Nothing, good monsieur, but to help Cavalery
Cobweb to scratch. I must to the barber's
monsieur, for methinks I am marvellous hairy   25

about the face. And I am such a tender ass, if my hair do but tickle me, I must scratch.

TITANIA

What, wilt thou hear some music, my sweet love?

BOTTOM

I have a reasonable good ear in music. Let's have the tongs and the bones.   30

TITANIA

Or say, sweet love, what thou desirest to eat.

BOTTOM

Truly, a peck of provender; I could munch your good dry oats. Methinks I have a great desire to a bottle of hay: good hay, sweet hay, hath no fellow.

TITANIA

I have a venturous fairy, that shall seek   35
The squirrel's hoard, and fetch thee thence new
    nuts.

BOTTOM

I had rather have a handful or two of dried peas. But I pray you, let none of your people stir me; I have an exposition of sleep come upon me.

TITANIA

Sleep thou, and I will wind thee in my arms.   40
Fairies, be gone, and be all ways away.

Exeunt Fairies.

So doth the woodbine the sweet honeysuckle
Gently entwist; the female ivy so
Enrings the barky fingers of the elm.
O, how I love thee! how I dote on thee!   45

They sleep.

Enter PUCK.

OBERON (*Coming forward*)
Welcome, good Robin: seest thou this sweet sight?
Her dotage now I do begin to pity;
For meeting her of late behind the wood,
Seeking sweet favours for this hateful fool,
I did upbraid her, and fall out with her.   50
For she his hairy temples then had rounded
With coronet of fresh and fragrant flowers;
And that same dew, which sometime on the buds
Was wont to swell like round and orient pearls,
Stood now within the pretty flowerets' eyes   55
Like tears that did their own disgrace bewail.
When I had at my pleasure taunted her,
And she in mild terms begged my patience,
I then did ask of her her changeling child;
Which straight she gave me, and her fairy sent   60
To bear him to my bower in fairy land.
And now I have the boy, I will undo
This hateful imperfection of her eyes.
And, gentle Puck, take this transforméd scalp,
From off the head of this Athenian swain,   65
That he awaking when the other do,
May all to Athens back again repair,
And think no more of this night's accidents
But as the fierce vexation of a dream.
But first I will release the Fairy Queen.   70

Touches TITANIA's *eyelids.*

Be as thou wast wont to be;
See as thou wast wont to see.
Dian's bud o'er Cupid's flower
Hath such force and blessed power.
Now, my Titania, wake you, my sweet Queen.   75

TITANIA (*Wakes and rises*)

My Oberon! What visions have I seen!
Methought I was enamoured of an ass.

OBERON

There lies your love.

TITANIA

             How came these things to pass?
O, how mine eyes do loathe his visage now!

OBERON

Silence awhile. Robin, take off this head;   80
Titania, music call, and strike more dead
Than common sleep, of all these five the sense.

TITANIA

Music, ho music, such as charmeth sleep!

Music plays.

PUCK

Now, when thou wak'st, with thine own fool's eyes
    peep.

OBERON

Sound, music; come, my Queen take hands with
    me,   85
And rock the ground whereon these sleepers be.
Now thou and I are new in amity,
And will tomorrow midnight solemnly
Dance in Duke Theseus' house triumphantly,
And bless it to all fair prosperity.   90
There shall the pairs of faithful lovers be
Wedded, with Theseus, all in jollity.

PUCK

Fairy King, attend and mark;
I do hear the morning lark.

OBERON

> Then, my Queen, in silence sad   95
> Trip we after the night's shade;
> We the globe can compass soon,
> Swifter than the wandering moon.

TITANIA

> Come, my lord, and in our flight
> Tell me how it came this night   100
> That I sleeping here was found,
> With these mortals on the ground.

Exeunt. The lovers and BOTTOM *sleep on.*

. . .

BOTTOM (*Waking up*)

When my cue comes, call me, and I will answer. My next is 'Most fair Pyramus'. Heigh-ho! Peter Quince! Flute the bellows-mender! Snout the 105 tinker! Starveling! God's my life! Stolen hence, and left me asleep! I have had a most rare vision. I have had a dream, past the wit of man to say what dream it was. Man is but an ass if he go about to expound this dream. Methought I was, – there 110 is no man can tell what. Methought I was, and methought I had – but man is but a patched fool, if he will offer to say what methought I had. The eye of man hath not heard, the ear of man hath not seen, man's hand is not able to taste, his 115 tongue to conceive, nor his heart to report, what my dream was. I will get Peter Quince to write a ballad of this dream; it shall be called 'Bottom's Dream', because it hath no bottom; and I will sing it in the latter end of a play, before the Duke. 120 Peradventure, to make it the more gracious, I shall sing it at her death.

Exit

1 Bottom and Titania are blissfully happy, but they make a very odd couple. Create two characters of your own: two people who are an unlikely match but who defy the world by being happy. Tell their story.

2 Oberon's power seems limitless. Do you think he uses his magic mischievously, or could he be dangerous? What if he hadn't decided to release Titania from the spell? What else could he have done?

3 Bottom says he will get Quince to write a ballad of his dream and call it 'Bottom's Dream'. A ballad is a song in verse which tells a story. See if you can write one or more verses for him.

Shakespeare's language

Shakespeare's stories of glory, passion, honour, sorrow, and all the deepest of human feelings, move each generation to marvel at his genius. But other writers have told good tales for the stage, and for the single silent reader curled up in a chair; and you might argue that you know of other gripping ones besides those of murdered Caesar, Romeo and Juliet, comical Malvolio and the desperate Macbeth. What is it, then, that makes Shakespeare 'bestride the narrow world like a Colossus' (as Cassius says of Caesar)? Why does everybody know his name, even if they have never read or seen one of his plays? What makes us fall under his spell?

He is England's greatest poet, and some people say that he is the greatest poet that the world has ever known. He used the language and the writing conventions of his day and drew them to new heights; magically weaving the musicality of his verse with deft and practical prose, inventing new words and creating new worlds of such dramatic power that he filled the theatres with excited audiences, and he still does.

Exploring his use of language helps us to enjoy his plays, as we see something of how they 'work'.

Blank verse

Plays written for the late sixteenth- and early seventeenth-century theatre were mostly written in a patterned form of poetry called 'blank verse': that is, rhythmic lines without a rhyme. Blank verse had a regular rhythm of ten syllables to a line; an unstressed syllable followed by a stressed syllable. (Examples of words with one syllable are 'is', 'and', 'but'; an easy example of a word with two syllables in which the second is stressed is 'today'.)

Here is an example of blank verse – Macbeth cries to the witches:

> I conjure you, by that which you profess,
> Howe'er you come to know it, answer me:

Try reading these two lines to yourself: can you hear the pattern of stresses?

There are five stressed syllables to each line, and this verse is written in what is called iambic pentameter. Iambic is the technical term for a pair of syllables in which the first syllable is unstressed and the second stressed. 'Pent' means five (a pentagon has five sides). Of all the ways in which verse can be written, blank verse is closest to the natural rhythms of speech. Shakespeare uses it to move from the most ordinary lines of action to the moments of deepest feeling.

1 Find an example of blank verse from *Romeo and Juliet, Macbeth* and *Julius Caesar,* each time selecting three or four lines at the most.

Copy them out and underline the stressed syllables. Then show your examples to a partner and read them aloud, checking that you have chosen correctly, and hearing how they sound.

2 Choose an example of a character's lines written in blank verse that has particularly moved or excited you. You may have found them as you worked on the previous question, or you might like to look again at the scenes from those plays. Work with a partner and share your choices, listening to how they sound, exploring what makes them so good.

Prose

In *A Midsummer Night's Dream,* we can see that Titania and Oberon speak in blank verse. Shakespeare gives them nobility and majesty, and their speech reflects this. By contrast, the humble workmen speak in ordinary prose, and this contrast is especially marked when Titania and Bottom talk to each other.

TITANIA
　　Thou art as wise as thou art beautiful.
BOTTOM
　　Not so, neither; but if I had wit enough to get out of this
　　wood, I have enough to serve mine own turn.

It is nearly always the case that working people such as Bottom or the Nurse in *Romeo and Juliet* use the language of prose. But Shakespeare also uses prose for moments of startling directness for his principal characters. When Caesar decides to go to the Capitol, he says determinedly: 'Give me my robe, for I will go.'

1 Look at how the servants of the household speak in *Twelfth Night,* and how the ignoble Sir Toby Belch joins them. Contrast this with Olivia's musicality in the second extract (page 84). Find some good examples of blank verse and prose, especially where Shakespeare weaves them together, and copy out at least three of each, underlining the stresses in the verse and putting a clear 'P' for prose against the rest.

2 Look at the scenes from *Macbeth* to find another example of lines spoken by a central character, such as Caesar's on the previous page, when the stark simplicity of a thought or action is uttered not in verse but in prose.

3 There is a third example of how Shakespeare uses prose. You can find it in *The Merchant of Venice* (Act 3 Scene 1), when the news comes that Antonio's ships lie wrecked and he is now a ruined man. Salerio, Antonio's friend, ventures to suggest that this is now the least of Antonio's troubles. Shylock turns passionately on him, and he might roar, or spit, or whisper this reply:

SHYLOCK

Let him look to his bond! He was wont to call me usurer; let him look to his bond! He was wont to lend money for a Christian courtesy; let him look to his bond!

SALERIO

Why, I am sure, if he forfeit, thou wilt not take his flesh – what's *that* good for?

SHYLOCK

To bait fish withal; – if it will feed nothing else, it will feed my revenge. He hath disgraced me, and hindered me half a million – laughed at my losses, mocked at my gains, scorned my nation, thwarted my bargains, cooled my friends, heated mine enemies – and what's his reason? I am a Jew. Hath not a Jew eyes? hath not a Jew hands, organs, dimensions, senses, affections, passions? fed with the same food, hurt with the same weapons, subject to the same diseases, healed by the same means, warmed and cooled by the same winter and summer as a Christian is? If you prick us, do we not bleed? If you tickle us, do we not laugh? if you poison us, do we not die? – And if you wrong us, shall we not revenge? If we are like you in the rest, we will resemble you in that. If a Jew wrong a Christian, what is his humility? Revenge! If a

Christian wrong a Jew, what should his sufferance be by Christian example? Why, revenge! The villainy you teach me I will execute, and it shall go hard but I will better the instruction.

Why do you think Shakespeare writes Shylock's lines in prose?

There are certain rhythms none the less that you can pick up in this speech. Look at: 'laughed at my losses, mocked at my gains, scorned my nation . . . '. There is also a pattern of questions. Shylock covers a lot of ground in his passion, but he does so with a formidable sense of mounting repetition.

a) Find and write down the words and phrases that Shylock repeats.

b) Now do the same for the questions he asks.

c) If you had to highlight one word or question or statement on which Shylock's voice might rise in a climax, which would it be?

Rhyming couplets

Sometimes Shakespeare uses rhyming couplets. These are lines of the same length and pattern, two of which rhyme together. The witches in *Macbeth* use them very effectively.

1 Look at the first incantations of the three witches (pages 44–5): 'Round about the cauldron go . . . '; 'Fillet of a fenny snake . . .' and 'Scale of dragon, tooth of wolf . . . '. Read them aloud in small groups, taking a couplet each or in pairs. What is the effect of the couplets? Would the spells work in the same way without the pattern and the rhyme?

2 Oberon speaks in rhyming couplets in the second extract from *A Midsummer Night's Dream* (pages 115–17).

a) Copy out two examples.

b) Explain why you think he does so at this point in the play.

3 In the same scene, when Bottom wants to go to sleep, Titania softly lets him, looking at him lovingly (page 114). Make up a magical spell for sending someone to sleep that she might well use herself as Bottom drifts off.

Imagery

When Shakespeare wants to tell us that Caesar is a man of huge stature, power and presence, he describes him in a way that puts a picture in our minds of a gigantic statue that once stood near the harbour of Rhodes (an island in the Aegean Sea). This statue was called the Colossus; it was built round 280 BC and was almost as high as the Statue of Liberty in New York harbour today – a huge engineering feat for those times. It was destroyed by an earthquake, but not before it had been declared one of the seven wonders of the world.

This is what Cassius says (Act 1 Scene 2):

Why, man, he doth bestride the narrow world
Like a Colossus, and we petty men
Walk under his huge legs, and peep about
To find ourselves dishonourable graves.

By using the word 'Colossus', we are prompted to think of something huge and wonderful. This use of a word picture is called 'imagery'. With this image, by association, we see Caesar as one of the wonders of the world.

1 When Caesar hears that a lion has been seen, pacing the streets of Rome, he says (page 32):

> Danger knows full well
> That Caesar is more dangerous than he.
> We are two lions littered in one day,
> And I the elder and more terrible,
> And Caesar shall go forth.

What are we meant to think when Caesar uses this image of the lion to describe himself?

2 When Romeo first sees Juliet (page 37), he whispers to himself that it seems 'she hangs upon the cheek of night as a rich jewel in an Ethiop's ear', and she makes him think of 'a snowy dove trooping with crows . . . '.

a) What do these images suggest to us about how he sees her beauty?

b) Find another two images elsewhere in this scene which Romeo and Juliet use to picture their love to each other.

3 Blood, magic, beauty, rage, power – these are powerfully suggested throughout the scenes in this collection. With a partner, write each of these words on a separate piece of paper. Then brainstorm around them all the words and pictures that spring to your mind. Finally, create some images of your own.

Who said what?

....

1 Write down the names of the characters who speak the following lines, and the play that they come from. Try to do it without looking at the texts. Check your answers between pages 11 and 75, to see how well you did.

2 When you have finished, devise a test for a friend in your class. Work with the second set of texts between pages 84 and 117. You will need to look for lines that are roughly the lengths of those in the test below, and which are important in the development of the scene, or which show us something about the character who is speaking.

   a) Since Cassius first did whet me against Caesar
     I have not slept.

   b)   And, gentle friends,
     Let's kill him boldly, but not wrathfully;
     Let's carve him as a dish fit for the gods,
     Not hew him as a carcass fit for hounds.

   c) By my life, this is my lady's hand!

   d) Take then thy bond, take thou thy pound of flesh,
     But in the cutting it, if thou dost shed
     One drop of Christian blood, thy lands and goods
     Are (by the laws of Venice) confiscate
     Unto the state of Venice.

   e) Double, double, toil and trouble:
     Fire, burn; and cauldron, bubble.

   f) Tie up my love's tongue, bring him silently.

   g) I am content.

h) If this fall into thy hand, revolve!

i) Then live, Macduff: what need I fear of thee?

j) O she doth teach the torches to burn bright!

k) Cowards die many times before their deaths;
   The valiant never taste of death but once.

l) I see their knavery: this is to make an ass of me,
   to fright me, if they could.

m) What angel wakes me from my flowery bed?

n) The cause is in my will; I will not come.

o) The quality of mercy is not strained;
   It droppeth as the gentle rain from heaven
   Upon the place beneath.

p) Do not go forth today. Call it my fear
   That keeps you in the house and not your own.

q)   . . . by my soul I swear,
   There is no power in the tongue of man
   To alter me. I stay here on my bond.

r) How now, you secret, black and midnight hags!
   What is 't you do?

s) Will not the ladies be afeard of the lion?

t) I could marry this wench for this device.

u) This, by his voice, should be a Montague.
   Fetch me my rapier, boy.

v) Thou art as wise as thou art beautiful.

w) My only love sprung from my only hate!

x) I will smile; I will do every thing that thou wilt have me.

y) By the pricking of my thumbs,
   Something wicked this way comes.

z) . . . and I will sing, that they shall hear I am not afraid.

How to use quotations

Look again at the lines quoted in this section. Many of them can be useful for you when you are thinking and writing for yourself about these plays by Shakespeare. For example, if you wanted to say something about how troubled Brutus was about the murder, you could back up your point by referring to quotation a): 'Since Cassius first did whet me against Caesar I have not slept.' It would be difficult for someone to convince you that Brutus was untouched by what he was being asked to do; you can show that he clearly could not sleep because of his anxiety. In those quotations, a) to z), find evidence to support these statements:

- Caesar acts as if he is above everyone else. He doesn't feel the need to explain his actions.
- Sir Toby doesn't care about hurting Malvolio's feelings. He's full of glee at the fun of the situation.
- Juliet is quick to realise the seriousness and the danger of loving Romeo.
- Malvolio is hopelessly in love.
- Bottom tries to be brave, even when he is very bewildered indeed.

Now write a character description of at least one of these: Caesar, Sir Toby, Juliet, Malvolio or Bottom. Search through the scenes in this book to find evidence to support your views. You can say what you like, as long as you can back yourself up!

Dramatic effects

Playwrights build into their plays ways of making them dramatically powerful. As well as creating exciting characters and events, they use devices which increase the play's dramatic power, such as the 'aside'. This is when a character speaks to the audience, and it is done as if the other characters do not overhear what is said.

A director can intensify the sense of drama by the staging of this moment, deciding for example where someone stands or moves to, how he or she speaks the lines, and how the stage is lit.

Soliloquy

When a character speaks aloud to herself or himself on stage, this is called a soliloquy. It is a way of revealing that person's inner thoughts. One of the most famous soliloquies comes from Shakespeare's play *Hamlet*, when Hamlet says, with deep uncertainty about his life, 'To be, or not to be: that is the question.' (You will often find that people who don't know anything about the play or what those words mean will still be able to quote them.)

An example from the plays looked at in this book comes from *Macbeth*. When, towards the end, Macbeth is given the news that his wife is dead, he speaks these lines to himself:

She should have died hereafter;
There would have been a time for such a word.

Tomorrow, and tomorrow, and tomorrow,
Creeps in this petty pace from day to day,
To the last syllable of recorded time;
And all our yesterdays have lighted fools
The way to dusty death. Out, out, brief candle!
Life's but a walking shadow, a poor player
That struts and frets his hour upon the stage,
And then is heard no more; it is a tale
Told by an idiot, full of sound and fury,
Signifying nothing.

1 Read these lines aloud to a partner, trying different ways of speaking them to explore how he might be feeling. For example, is he angry? Or desperate? Or finished?

2 Why might Shakespeare have wanted Macbeth to speak to himself rather than to another person – say, the messenger who brought the news? In other words, how is the dramatic effect of this moment made more intense by a soliloquy at this point?

3 What is the effect of repeating the word 'tomorrow'?

4 Macbeth likens us to actors on a stage, strutting for an hour or so and then silenced. Why do you think he does this? What other word pictures or 'images' does he conjure up to represent life? Write down each one, explaining how it works, like this:

Quotation   . . . a poor player
                   That struts and frets his hour upon the stage,
                   And then is heard no more.
Image   People are likened to actors on a stage.
Meaning   Our lives aren't real, and don't have any
                   lasting meaning. We are acting out a part,
                   'strutting' and worrying until it is all over, and
                   then death silences us.

Here is another example of a soliloquy: it comes from *Julius Caesar* (Act 3 Scene 1). Mark Antony has seen Caesar's body, and is left alone with it after the conspirators leave, charged with giving them public support when the time comes to meet the people. He says he will, and then privately and in anguish expresses the fullness of his grief and rage:

> O pardon me, thou bleeding piece of earth,
> That I am meek and gentle with these butchers.
> Thou art the ruins of the noblest man
> That ever livéd in the tide of times.
> Woe to the hand that shed this costly blood!
> Over thy wounds now do I prophesy, –
> Which like dumb mouths do ope their ruby lips,
> To beg the voice and utterance of my tongue –
> A curse shall light upon the limbs of men;
> Domestic fury and fierce civil strife
> Shall cumber all the parts of Italy;
> Blood and destruction shall be so in use,
> And dreadful objects so familiar,
> That mothers shall but smile when they behold
> Their infants quartered with the hands of war,
> All pity choked with custom of fell deeds;
> And Caesar's spirit ranging for revenge,
> With Até by his side, come hot from hell,
> Shall in these confines, with a monarch's voice
> Cry 'Havoc!' and let slip the dogs of war,
> That this foul deed shall smell above the earth
> With carrion men, groaning for burial.

Prepare a reading of this soliloquy. Think carefully about what is said and why. Explore your conclusions with a partner, and then deliver it to the class (or ask them to listen to a tape of your interpretation).

Oration

'Oratory' is carefully chosen, elaborate public speech to
persuade and inspire an audience. The language is used
for maximum effect, and Shakespeare's oratory in verse
form can be deeply persuasive. Fine examples can be
found in *Julius Caesar*, when Brutus and Mark Antony vie
with each other for the support and confidence of the
crowd after Caesar has died (Act 3 Scene 2). Look at
Antony's speech below:

> If you have tears, prepare to shed them now.
> You all do know this mantle. I remember
> The first time ever Caesar put it on.
> 'T was on a summer's evening in his tent,
> That day he overcame the Nervii.
> Look, in this place ran Cassius' dagger through;
> See what a rent the envious Casca made;
> Through this, the well-belovéd Brutus stabbed,
> And, as he plucked his curséd steel away,
> Mark how the blood of Caesar followed it,
> As rushing out of doors, to be resolved
> If Brutus so unkindly knocked, or no;
> For Brutus, as you know, was Caesar's angel.
> Judge, O you gods, how dearly Caesar loved him!
> This was the most unkindest cut of all.
> For when the noble Caesar saw him stab,
> Ingratitude, more strong than traitors' arms,
> Quite vanquished him; then burst his mighty heart,
> And in his mantle muffling up his face,
> Even at the base of Pompey's statuë,
> Which all the while ran blood, great Caesar fell.
> O what a fall was there, my countrymen!
> Then I, and you, and all of us fell down,
> Whilst bloody treason flourished over us.
> O now you weep, and I perceive you feel

The dint of pity. These are gracious drops.
Kind souls, what weep you, when you but behold
Our Caesar's vesture wounded? Look you here!
Here is himself, marred, as you see, with traitors.

1 Take it in turns with a partner to read the speech, getting a feel of how it might sound.

2 Antony's first words tell us in what mood he wants to leave the crowd. Is he speaking in poetry or prose? How can you tell? What is the effect of this opening?

3 'You all do know this mantle.' This makes Caesar's cloak seem familiar. What is Antony appealing to in the minds of the people?

4 'I remember . . . ' – this is almost conversational; 'a summer's evening . . . ' – this has a soft sound to it. What is Antony saying in these two sentences about his own relationship with Caesar? Why should that matter to the crowd?

5 What is the effect of using the verbs 'Look', 'See' and 'Judge' at the beginning of three of the lines?

6 Antony chooses a particular image to describe Brutus. What is it, and how does it work to make his point?

7 Antony is reeling the crowd in like fishes on a line. What is his final flourish?

8 How would you say that final word? Would you spit it out? Let it trail away? Shout it?

9 Look at a copy of the play to see how the crowd responds. What are the dangers of oratory?

Bringing the play to life on stage

A playhouse such as the Globe, with the curved shell of its walls open to the sky, and its main stage jutting out into the standing audience, was unlike most of our box-shaped theatres today. You can read a more detailed description of the old playhouses on page 3. We are used to sitting in front of a stage, where curtains sweep down between acts and rise to reveal new scenery, although modern theatres can also be found above pubs, in schools and in converted buildings – such as the old cotton exchange in Manchester – where directors try out the effects of differently shaped stages and spaces for the audience. Shakespeare sometimes had to plan the performance of a play to fit in the shape of a large room in a private house.

But wherever a play is seen, in whatever period, you can be sure of two things: that the stage is of crucial importance in how a play can be presented, and the person directing it will bring along very personal ideas about what should happen. Sometimes, the fewer the options open to a director, the more powerfully she or he is forced to rely on the writer's words: so it isn't always a question of how big a place is, or how many ways you can light it, or whether there is room and money for elaborate sets. Though it can be fun spending lots of money on these things, it can also be fun, and sometimes even more challenging, to produce a play on a tight budget in a tiny room.

Directing

Imagine that you are the director of at least two of the following scenes. (If you want to, you could work as a co-director with someone else.)

For one, you are an Elizabethan, with torches and flares, musicians and boy actors, cannons and trap-doors, and the rich modern language of that new playwright, Shakespeare, to help you. Try to get into the mind of such a person: search in your school or local library for some pictures of the old playhouses, or of the modern Globe in London, and study how they looked. Think about the possibilities of split-level stages, and the fun (and the drawbacks!) of having an audience ready to wade in and contribute their reactions.

For another, you are a director today. Perhaps you've had a telephone call – your big chance has come! You have a huge budget and the most sensational of actors and actresses desperate to star in your production. Or perhaps your position is less glamorous, but you're teaming with ideas. Generations have heard of Shakespeare: now they are going to see him your way.

Here are the moments from your key scenes. You may have to concentrate on just one or two characters, or you may have to decide how you will present and control a crowd scene.

1 Caesar's death.
2 Romeo sees Juliet.
3 Malvolio finds the letter.
4 Shylock loses his case.
5 Macbeth sees the witches.
6 Bottom discovers the reactions of his friends to his new appearance.

Create a special folder for this work, with an appropriate cover.

When you begin:

a) Find the lines, and copy them out.

b) In the margin of your script, write notes which will help the speaker to deliver the lines. You could write 'sadly', or 'working up to being angry', or 'softly' . . . whatever strikes you as right.

c) Draw a diagram of the actors' movements on your stage, using arrows to show where they should begin and where they should end up.

d) Write notes to indicate any lighting or special effects you want that you have it in your power to use.

e) As a modern director, decide who you want to play the parts. Give reasons for your choice, explaining what these actors and actresses could bring to your production. Make sure with the kind of production you are putting on that you can afford them.

Set design and costumes

For the modern director, there are some further considerations: Whether or not you have a lot of money or a little, you will need to work out what sets and costumes will suit your production.

Often Shakespeare's plays have been set in his own times; everything has an Elizabethan 'feel', firmly placing the production in that era. Other directors have chosen to set his plays in another period of history. *Julius Caesar*, for example, has been set in Nazi Germany during World War II: this has underlined what the play has to say about the dangers of power and politics. *Romeo and Juliet* has been set in the present day, pointing out the ever-present conflicts between the generations.

Decide what period in history best suits your interpretation of the play's message, and then you can decide about your sets and costumes.

Advertising

There are lots of options open to you to advertise your production.

Design a poster. You could bring out the horror and the supernatural if your play is *Macbeth*; perhaps stricken love if it is *Romeo and Juliet* . . . decide how you want to draw the attention of passers-by. Your idea may also link in with the cover picture on the programmes sold in the theatre, which you could design at the same time.

You might be able to afford advertising at peak TV viewing time. If you had two minutes in which to put your message across, what would you show? What would you say? You could hold a meeting about this, and brainstorm the views of a handful of others. Then with your team, create the ad.

Reviews

You have had your first night and the critics are wild about it! They rave about the acting, the sets, the atmosphere, your understanding of the story . . . and you are so pleased that you cut out and frame one of the reviews. Put on your writer's hat and write the review you would love to read.

Compare the productions

Now compare your two productions. Look back at your plans, describing how you came to your decisions. You could think along the following lines, and call this piece of writing: 'Myself as Director'.

- Was it hard getting into the mind of an Elizabethan director?

- Modern directors have more options open to them; did this make the job easier or harder?

- Was anything especially tricky to work out?

- Was anything particularly successful?

- Were you better working with others or happier thinking things out on your own?

- Do you think you kept within your budget?

- Is there another play you'd like to put on?

- What kind of director would you like to be known as – cheerful? Difficult to work for but still rewarding? Full of ideas? Providing strong leadership, or keen to hear others' points of view? Having a particular view about life that you'd like to put across in your plays?

The background to the plays

Witchcraft

Macbeth and *A Midsummer Night's Dream* both contain magic. In Shakespeare's time, more than 2,000 people – perhaps many more – were put to death after accusations of witchcraft. The word 'witch' comes from the Anglo-Saxon word 'wicca' meaning 'wise one' and originally a witch was either a man or a woman who supposedly had supernatural powers. Through the years, however, only women came to be seen as witches, and sometimes innocent old women who lived alone came under suspicion and were subjected to crude 'tests' to see if they were innocent or guilty. See what you can find out.

Ancient Rome

Shakespeare's audience would have known about the Roman Empire, which, at the height of its power, controlled most of Europe, including England, parts of Asia and northern Africa.

According to legend, Rome was first ruled by a king in 750 BC, but eventually it became a Republic. It was governed by the Senate, whose members were drawn from noble families and were known as Patricians. The Senate elected two consuls from their midst who were very powerful, and Caesar was one of them. He ruled firstly with two others, Pompey and Marcus Crassus, in what was known as the Triumvirate. How he came to be sole ruler is a gripping story, and it is this story that provides the background to the conspirators' decision to murder him.

See what you can find out about this story. You could also find out about any other aspect of life in Ancient Rome that interests you.

Shylock and the history of the Jews

Anti-Semitic feelings (prejudice against Jewish people) were rife at the time in which *The Merchant of Venice* is set. Shakespeare was drawing on a well-established hatred when he made Shylock rage against its injustice. Anti-Semitism reached a peak in the twentieth century with the Holocaust: the terrible attempt by Hitler in World War II to do away with the Jewish race. You may know of *The Diary of Anne Frank*: an account written by a young girl of her family's efforts to survive the German persecution, by hiding, only to be discovered at the last and taken to concentration camps. All but her father died, and Anne's diary is a testimony to their experience and their courage.

There is a lot of literature now and a great deal of media coverage of this particular form of racial hatred. You could find out for yourself what happened in history and is happening now. Or you could think about other victims of racial prejudice and find out about their history and their present lives.

Shakespeare's world

Poverty, disease and death in the streets . . . riches, glamour and intrigue at the court of Queen Elizabeth I and then King James – the lives of the poor and the rich were very different in Shakespeare's lifetime. He would have seen both at first hand. He would have known about the ideas of the astronomers Galileo (in Italy) and Kepler (in Germany) who demonstrated that Copernicus' theory in 1543 was right: the earth is not the centre of the universe, but the earth and the other planets revolve around the sun. He would have known about the voyages of Sir Francis Drake, opening up a new world to British people, and of the Gunpowder Plot – Guy Fawkes' attempt to blow up the House of Lords on 5 November 1605. What a time to be alive! And to be able to watch Shakespeare's plays on stage just after he'd written them . . .

Find out about life in his times: take an incident that happened then, or a person who became famous for something, or simply look at what it might have been like to live an ordinary life as a boy or girl in the town or the country, sometime between 1564, when Shakespeare was born, and 1616 when he died.

Shakespeare's life

We know some things about Shakespeare: where he was born, for instance (Stratford-upon-Avon in Warwickshire), and who his parents were. He went to a school that you can still see today. We know that he married and had a daughter and then twins, and went to London where he probably joined one of the city's theatre companies which presented a variety of plays week after week. Somehow, his ordinary life took an extraordinary turn and he became the man whose name rings down the centuries as the greatest and the most loved writer the world has ever known. Find out what you can about his life. There are some certain facts and some interesting theories.

Issues for discussion

Shakespeare's plays raise a number of issues that are relevant to us today. Four of them are listed below. With each one that your teacher and class decides to think about, it may help you to work in small groups first, using the ideas outlined as starting points. Someone can take notes while you talk, and another person can report back to the whole class. Then everyone can have a chance to discuss together the most interesting points, and you could write about your thoughts and conclusions afterwards.

1 Julius Caesar, Dictator of Rome, is murdered by Brutus and his co-conspirators. They think it is the right thing to do.

Is it ever right to kill the leader of a nation?

Consider:

- Is it ever right to kill anyone?
- What if the leader is a man like Hitler?
- Can you think of anyone in your own lifetime who has abused his or her power?
- Who do you know of who has reason to fear murder by some of his or her own people?
- Is there a difference between Macbeth (whose first act after imagining himself as King of Scotland was to kill the reigning king, Duncan) and Brutus and the other conspirators who killed Caesar?
- Do proper elections in a democratic country work as a check to violence against leaders?

- Do you think the murders of Duncan and Caesar could happen in your own country today?

2 Romeo and Juliet are forced apart by their parents, not just because the two families have a history of hating each other. Juliet's parents have another marriage arranged for her, and they believe they have the right to insist that she does as she's told.

Do parents have a right to a say in whom their child marries?

Consider:

- Parents have more experience than their children: can that experience be useful?

- As parents watch their children grow and change through various stages, could they help prevent the possibility of an unhappy marriage taking place?

- Some cultures have arranged marriages and many couples are very happy and successful as a result. Is choosing a partner always a very private and individual matter which not even friends can necessarily help with?

- If things go wrong between partners, does it always have to lead to divorce?

- Might Romeo and Juliet have fallen out of love anyway? Should they have listened to their families?

- Could their story happen today?

3 Both Malvolio in *Twelfth Night* and Bottom in *A Midsummer Night's Dream* are teased. Both men are easy targets: their natural characters lend themselves to mockery. Bottom simply wonders at his curious 'dream' afterwards, but Malvolio cannot accept for a moment that he might have brought anything on himself.

Some people think it never hurts to make fun of someone, especially if you don't mean any harm. Is this true?

Consider:

- Some people can be over-sensitive; is it important to have a sense of humour?

- Does it matter more if someone feels publicly embarrassed rather than just hurt inside?

- Are some people natural bullies? Can anything be done about them?

- What about situations in which some people keep quiet because they're afraid to stand up and say, 'Let's stop!' even though they know that things are getting out of hand? Can peer pressure be strong?

- Do you think Malvolio's feelings were hurt? Or do you think he deserved what happened to him?

- Did Oberon and Puck succeed in making a fool out of Bottom?

- Are some subjects 'off-limits' for jokes – too serious or too personal to be funny?

4 When Antonio is saved at the trial, it seems like a victory for goodness and justice. Shylock's bond was a sinister and frightening one. But what about the background to this story? What about Shylock's life, lived in the shadow of anti-Semitism, the age-old racist feelings against Jewish people? Nobody in the court said anything about that.

Most people think that racism is wrong but that you can't hope to get rid of it completely. It seems to be a fact of life. Is this your view? Or do you feel more positive?

Consider:

- Are there any groups of people whom you think are most likely to experience racism and/or have a history of racism?

- Are there certain types of people who are racist? Do you think it would be true to say that everyone has to ask themselves if they are racist in any way?
- Are there certain places – the inner cities for example – where people are more likely to meet with racism? Or could you find it anywhere?
- What forms can racism take?
- How can schools help to change society? How can they fail?
- How can families make a difference?
- Can you understand Shylock's rage? What about the lengths to which he took his anger? Was he punished too much? Does his punishment tell us anything about how the people of Venice regarded victims of racism?

Persuade me!

Choose two members of the class to act out each of the following confrontations between characters. The rest of the class can then 'hot-seat' them, firing questions to see if their views can stand up to pressure. You could take a vote at the end to see who has been the most convincing.

a) Shylock versus (against) Antonio, over the matter of the bond: the 'pound of flesh'.

b) Macbeth versus Macduff: a king has the right to protect his position against all comers.

c) Malvolio versus Sir Toby Belch; the household steward versus the knight. Do servants have rights? If so, what are they?

d) Romeo versus Juliet's father: Romeo would make a good husband for Capulet's daughter.

e) Bottom versus Oberon: a worthy if foolish workman is of more value than any king.

f) Caesar versus Brutus. Who is the better man? The great and powerful Dictator, with some human failings, or 'the noblest Roman of them all'? (You might be interested to know that E.M. Forster, a famous modern writer, once said: 'I hate the idea of causes, and if I had to choose between betraying my country and betraying my friend, I hope I should have the guts to betray my country.')

Everyone can prepare for this. You should think carefully and jot down some notes on these points:

- What has the character done?
- What happens to her/him?

- What is the background to these events?
- Are there any 'mitigating circumstances' – a term lawyers use when they look for reasons to excuse a person's actions?
- What would you do in this person's place?
- How do you feel about her/him at the moment?

The two characters themselves can prepare a defence along these lines, and should be ready to explain the reasons for their decisions, arguing their positions forcefully.

Comparisons

Two characters: Macduff and Brutus

When Macbeth uses his new power against his country, murdering anyone who stands in his way, Macduff gets ready to oppose him. As a general in the former king's army, he is unafraid to fight, but wants to fight only for a just cause. When his wife and children are murdered by Macbeth, he needs no further spurring on.

The conspirators in the Senate in Rome are equally convinced that Caesar is too powerful. Brutus only reluctantly joins them, for such extreme action gnaws at his conscience, then he too is persuaded and embarks on a fight to the end.

1 How would Brutus explain himself to history, to the generations to come? Write the letter that he might have left to us before his death, accounting for his decision and what it felt like to have made it.

2 Now imagine that Macduff is holding a book in his hand which relates the history of Caesar's times, and which contains a copy of the letter Brutus wrote: his version of the murder and the part that he personally played. Write Macduff's thoughts as he thinks about the ways in which their lives have moved towards a similar conclusion – that sometimes good men must contemplate acts that go against their natural character.

Two characters: Bottom and Malvolio

Bottom in *A Midsummer Night's Dream* and Malvolio in *Twelfth Night* are both teased. Bottom is given an ass's head and Malvolio is made to feel a fool. Which of them gets the worse deal? Is it just a question of what happens to them, or is it also a case of how they respond to those events?

1. Work with a partner: one of you can be a friend of Bottom, indignantly supporting him and describing what happened. The other can account for how outrageously Malvolio has been treated.

2. Swop your arguments with another pair; look at each other's work and see who has put the most convincing case. Then check around the class to see if the same conclusions have been reached.

Two places: the heathland in *Macbeth* and the wood in *A Midsummer Night's Dream*

Both places have a sense that the day's warmth has vanished, replaced with something other than the natural temperature of the earth; that silence alternates with rustlings; that magical powers are at work, distorting shapes and conjuring visions that would terrify you if you were there alone.

1. Describe what you might see and hear if you were in the wood, and how you might feel.

2. Now do the same for the wild heathland of Macbeth's Scotland.

3 Which place has given you a stronger sense of danger, and why?

Themes

The theme of power runs through *Julius Caesar* and *Macbeth*. It is interesting to look at how Macbeth is seen to use his power when he is newly crowned King of Scotland, and how Brutus and the others fear that Caesar will use his. You can also see immense power at work in the way that Oberon uses his magic. There are other themes which run through two or more of the extracts from the six plays in this book.

1 Look at the following themes and write down three that interest you:

power   magic   justice   prejudice   love
loyalty   honour   anger   blame

2 a) Taking the first of your three themes, jot down the names of the plays in which you find it.

b) Jot down the names of characters through which this theme is expressed.

c) Jot down the places and events associated with it.

d) Copy out any lines from the texts that support your view that these plays address this theme. Here is an example of how your notes could look:

Magic	
A Midsummer Night's Dream	*Macbeth*
Oberon	The witches
Woodland	Wild heathland
O's magic affects Titania	Ws' magic affects Macbeth
• 'Be as thou wast wont to be; See as thou wast wont to see.' – O's magic power over her	• see spells

e) Now use your notes to write a detailed description of the ways in which these plays express this theme, showing how they do this similarly and differently. You might want to say, for example, that the witches' magic seems more deadly than Oberon's; that he teases, but they have to do with death.

f) Do this for the two other themes you have chosen.

Further ideas for coursework

Twelfth Night

1 Illyria is an imaginary world. Directors have had fun deciding whether it is English, Italian, French, Russian . . . One Stratford production in 1987 had sets which made Illyria look like a 'sun-kissed, white-walled, travel-brochure Greek island'. Where would you put Illyria? What clues would you give your audience in the set? After thinking and talking with a partner, produce a set design for your own production of *Twelfth Night*, and then write about how you came to your decision, giving your reasons.

2 Is Malvolio doomed to failure because he is not a 'hero'? What do you expect a hero to look and be like? Write about heroes you know in real life and in books, plays and films, and show how you think Malvolio fits or doesn't fit into this category.

Julius Caesar

1 The crowd is like a beast with many heads. It moves and murmurs like a single creature. What does it contribute to the play?

2 The main event in this play is the death of Caesar, and the play is called after him. The scene before the murder concentrates on the anguished inner feelings of Brutus. The play continues to reveal the sorrow and despair of

Mark Antony. Who do you think the play is about? Explain your reasons.

3 Script and direct a scene in which Brutus and Antony privately confront each other. Write up afterwards how you arrived at your ideas, and what it was like to see your work in action as your actors interpreted the script.

Romeo and Juliet

1 Romeo was to blame for everything that happened; after all, he started it off by gatecrashing the Capulet's ball. Do you agree?

2 The last two lines of the play are:

> For never was a story of more woe
> Than this of Juliet and her Romeo.

Do you think this is a story ONLY about unhappiness?

3 There are at least three celebrated film versions of this story:

- Zeffirelli's *Romeo and Juliet,* beautiful and heartbreaking
- *West Side Story* – an American, musical version set in the twentieth century which has become a classic, updating the play's message
- an animated version of some Russian film-makers with the BBC.

There is also a version of the story in novel form, set in Ireland and written by Joan Linguard. See what you can get hold of and then compare one or two of them, describing what they contribute to your understanding of Shakespeare's play.

Macbeth

1 Shakespeare's main historical source for the story was the 1587 edition of Holinshed's *Chronicles of England, Scotland, and Ireland*, which he had already used for his history plays. Shakespeare changed the picture of Macbeth, setting aside Holinshed's praise of Macbeth as a ruler who was intent on maintaining justice, giving the country 'commendable laws' and punishing 'all enormities and abuse'. Holinshed also suggested that Macbeth had some proper claims to the throne. But Shakespeare makes him into an almost totally brutal king. Consider:

- Which version of Macbeth's character do you prefer?
- Which other characters have you met in plays or films who are created as total 'baddies'? Do any of them have any redeeming features? (Does Macbeth?) Which kind of character is the more interesting – the 'all bad' or the 'somewhat mixed'?

Describe and compare these characters, including Macbeth. Work out what makes some characters in stories in books or plays exciting and compelling and some not very interesting.

2 Take the basic plot of *Macbeth:*

- A general in the king's army, hissed on by witches, grabs the throne for himself.
- The king's death is quickly followed by the deaths of others. Macbeth murderously moves forward, eliminating his enemies.
- Lady Macbeth also dies, desperate and overcome after having fully shared her husband's grisly ambitions.
- Macbeth, alone, exhausted and in anguish, is killed by the forces of goodness. Macduff arrives with help from England and peace is restored to Scotland.

Update this story, setting it in modern times in your own country. You could write it as a play or a story. Make sure that your central character, like Macbeth, begins to understand the cost of his actions.

A Midsummer Night's Dream

1 What should Oberon and Titania look like? Would you like them to look very different from the humans? Should they be different from each other or very alike? Look at photos from past productions and illustrations from different editions of the play. Think about how they each come across in the scenes you know well. Then design their costumes, and write up the reasons for your decisions.

2 Do either Bottom or Oberon learn a lesson from this night spent in the wood? Describe what happens to them and what they do as a result.

3 Imagine you are Quince and that the director of another actors' company asks you whether Bottom is a good actor and a good member for the group. What would you say? Write a reference for Bottom, giving your opinions. You should say what he is capable of and what his special contributions are. Give some evidence and sum up your feelings in a last vivid and punchy sentence.

The Merchant of Venice

1 Portia has to dress as a man in order to speak in court. Her thinking, her sensitive judgement and natural authority win the case. Imagine that you are a journalist, sitting in court that day. You know who she is and long to tell all of Venice. Write a description of her that will sell copies like hot cakes the next day.

2 Portia's speech and Shylock's exit are two major moments in the courtroom scene. If you were filming this scene, how would you instruct the camera operators? You might want to pan the camera around on the characters' faces as they listened to Portia: if so, you would have to divide the lines up according to how they might make an impact on each individual there. You might want to take the focus repeatedly back to Shylock, or you might want to keep Portia at the heart of the scene . . . What do you think?

The six plays

1 Take a feeling: sadness, loneliness, despair, anger, hope or joy. Then take two or more characters from the six plays and show how they embody this feeling. Describe what happens and compare how they react.

2 Think of the best moment for you in any two or more plays. Then think of some music which would go well with them. If you like the witches' scene in *Macbeth*, you might be able to think of some weird and frightening music to accompany their first appearance. A love song by a band you like might suit the point when Romeo moves across the room to Juliet. You might need to turn the volume up and down to suit your dramatic purposes. Perhaps you could make a tape of both speaking voices and music. Then explain in writing what makes these choices the right ones.